THE WINT
VEGETARI

THE WINTER VEGETARIAN

Stephanie Segal

Illustrated by
Annette Lewin

PAPERMAC

First published 1989 by
PAPERMAC
a division of Macmillan Publishers Limited
4 Little Essex Street London WC2R 3LF
and Basingstoke

Associated companies in Auckland, Delhi, Dublin, Gaborone, Hamburg, Harare, Hong
Kong, Johannesburg, Kuala Lumpur, Lagos, Manzini, Melbourne, Mexico City, Nairobi,
New York, Singapore and Tokyo

ISBN 0-333-48101-1

Typeset by Rowland Phototypesetting Limited
Bury St Edmunds, Suffolk
Printed by Billings Bookplan, Worcester

This book is dedicated to
the memory of my much loved aunt
Queenie Fleishman
who would have loved the recipes.

CONTENTS

ACKNOWLEDGMENTS

I would like to thank my friends and their families for trying recipes and giving me their time and comments. My special thanks to Georgina Liveras who spent a lot of time trying recipes, reading the manuscript, and tactfully offering constructive criticism and giving me much needed support in this project. It seems very easy to write a cookery book until you do it!

Thank you to John, Hagai, Gilad and Yoav who gave me lots of encouragement and help with the book, who ate the food and made many comments, not all repeated here!

I would also like to thank the wonderful staff of Church End Library, Finchley, who helped me in my research and were always willing to find any material needed.

The Fresh Fruit and Vegetable Information Bureau and the British Food Information Bureau publish information on fruit and vegetables which has been very helpful.

INTRODUCTION

In the last few years, there has been an enormous increase in vegetarian eating in the Western world. More and more young people are cutting out meat from their diets, and recent publicity exposing the dangers of salmonella and listeria together with a growing public awareness of the more unacceptable aspects of meat production are convincing people of the benefits of eating vegetarian food.

Vast numbers of new cookery books are published each year, yet to many people vegetarian cooking seems complicated and difficult. Sometimes ingredients required are hard to obtain, while, paradoxically, vegetables and fruits found in most supermarkets do not appear amongst vegetarian recipes.

I have for many years searched for books catering for the different seasons, particularly recipes for the more unusual vegetables and fruits. I adore the food of the Mediterranean and the Middle East where vegetables and grains are used in the most imaginative ways and are not always smothered in Cheddar cheese.

In this book I have introduced new recipes for winter vegetables and fruits, as well as a few old favourites, together with some nutritional information. Each recipe provides very generous portions for four. There are thirty-one recipes in each section: starters, soups, main courses and desserts, one for each day of the month and a comprehensive range for the season. I hope that this will be the first of a seasonal series.

Bon appétit!

SOME POINTS FOR YOU TO BEAR IN MIND WHEN YOU READ THIS BOOK

Quantities

All recipes in this book are for very generous portions for four people.

Olive oil

I always use olive oil in preference to other types of oil or butter, primarily for its superb taste but also for health reasons. Olive oil is rich in mono-unsaturates. Recent research has shown that diets high in olive oil (such as in many Mediterranean countries) can reduce cholesterol levels and may help to reduce the likelihood of heart disease and high blood pressure. Its only disadvantage is that it does contain a high number of calories. The history of olive oil can be traced back to ancient times when it was used medicinally to lower blood pressure, among other things, and as a massage oil for Greek athletes.

Each pressing of olive oil is classified, with extra virgin being the top classification and the most expensive. Olive oil that has been cold pressed is also considered superior to others.

As olive oil is expensive, I always use two types. I use the extra virgin for salad dressings and cooking when the flavour of the oil is essential to the taste of the dish. For more general cooking, I use a less expensive Italian pure olive oil which is thinner. Do try different types of olive oil to find your own favourite. French, Greek, Italian and Spanish olive oils of the same classification taste totally different, depending on the region's soil and climate.

I have seldom included exact quantities of olive oil in the recipes because the amount required varies tremendously according to the vegetables, the type of saucepan used and whether you cook on gas or electricity. Coat the saucepan with a thin layer of oil and you can always add more if necessary. You will gradually develop a natural feel for the amount to use.

Herbs and seasonings

Feel free to add more garlic, herbs and seasonings to any of the recipes. My grandmother never used scales, measuring spoons or jugs in her life; she cooked by instinct and taste, an attitude I heartily recommend.

Experiment, too, with different herbs and combinations of herbs. They can revolutionise the taste of any dish. Try some of the recipes using different herbs and see what a difference they make to the flavour of the finished dish.

I like to grow my own herbs as the taste is so much superior to dried herbs but I also buy the frozen tubs of herbs now stocked by many supermarkets. In order of preference, use fresh, frozen or dried herbs. Make sure dried herbs are stored in airtight jars or the aroma will quickly disappear and become musty. Try to buy the flat-leaved Mediterranean parsley (rather than the curly English variety) and fresh coriander, which are highly aromatic and really do transform food. Some supermarkets now stock them but I prefer to buy them at Italian, Greek or Asian grocers where turnover is more frequent and the herbs are therefore likely to be fresher.

In certain recipes I have used turmeric or saffron to produce a natural yellow colour. Saffron has a more delicate colour and flavour, but is also much more expensive than turmeric, which is particularly good with rice. The two are interchangeable in all the recipes.

Stocks

I don't like to use stocks of any description (and certainly not those made with stock cubes). In some recipes, particularly soups, stock is needed and I generally use shoyu or tamari sauces which can be bought in all health food shops and some supermarkets. These are both natural soya sauces, rich in natural protein and essential minerals. Shoyu is not as strong as tamari so try both and see which one you prefer. I NEVER buy regular soya sauce. Most brands available contain vast amounts of artificial preservatives and colouring (they also taste awful). Yeast extract (such as Marmite) is another good substitute which produces a very strong flavour. If you don't like the taste of any of these, use a vegetable stock (see page 51). Many vegetarian cooks use miso to make stock, which is a soya bean, rice or barley fermented paste, available in health food shops. It is full of essential nutrients, but is an acquired taste. Try a small quantity and see if you like it.

Cream and yoghourt

In several recipes I have suggested using cream or yoghourt. If you don't like using cream for health reasons, substitute yoghourt, which will produce a very similar effect. I normally use Greek yoghourt. If you want to cut down your dairy intake, buy Greek sheep's milk yoghourt which has an unusual, but pleasant, taste. When adding cream or yoghourt to soups, do not let the soup boil or they will curdle. For the dessert dishes, use live yoghourt, Greek yoghourt or try one of the French skimmed milk cheeses now widely available.

Rice

In preference to ordinary rice, I like to use wild rice, which is not in fact a real rice but a wild grass. It has the most wonderful taste and is very nutritious, although it is expensive. To make it go further use half wild rice and half regular long grain rice to make the quantity specified in the recipe. It combines very well, particularly with brown rice, and gives a more complex, nutty flavour. Wild rice is widely available in health food shops and many supermarkets.

Pulses

Pulses are invaluable in vegetarian cookery and are full of protein. A wide selection can be obtained in health food shops. All pulses should be soaked for several hours, preferably overnight, which will reduce the cooking time and allow any small pieces of grit to rise to the surface. Drain and wash thoroughly before cooking. The only exception to this rule are red lentils which do not need prior soaking.

When cooking, beans, in particular, must be boiled for ten minutes before the heat is reduced to a simmer.

Tahini

Tahini (sometimes known as tahina) is a sesame seed paste which makes a good starter and is much used in Middle Eastern cookery. It is widely available in supermarkets, health food shops and Greek or Jewish grocers. Buy the tahini in glass jars as its flavour is much better than the tinned variety.

5

Avocado

There are many different types of avocado but I find that the ones with the best taste are the small black crinkly skinned Hass variety. To test if an avocado is ripe, cradle it in your hand and it should give slightly to the touch. If your fingers sink in too deeply it is probably overripe. If the avocado is hard you can ripen it at home by placing it in a sealed brown paper bag with an onion or a potato for twenty-four hours. There is a chemical explanation for this, which, being somewhat unscientific, I have forgotten, but it really does work. You can use a plastic bag, too, but it works best with brown paper.

A bonus of avocados is that the stones make lovely houseplants. Wash the stone thoroughly and place the rounded end into a yoghourt pot filled with water. Support it with toothpicks on each side, pushed through the pot and the stone. As soon as healthy roots appear, plant in soil and take care not to overwater. It will eventually grow into a tall plant.

Filo Pastry

Filo pastry (sometimes called strudel or phillo) is widely available frozen in supermarkets and is sometimes stocked fresh in Cypriot or Greek food shops. There are two important rules when cooking with filo pastry:
1. It must never be allowed to dry out. Once defrosted, wrap it in a damp teacloth until it is all used up. I start using it before it is completely defrosted so that it doesn't get too dry and it is very pliable at that stage.
2. Each layer of filo must be lavishly brushed with butter. This is essential or else the pastry will dry out when baking.

Tofu

Tofu is soybean curd, looking rather like a slab of thick white cheese, and is enormously adaptable in cookery. It can be used instead of eggs in many recipes and is excellent in quiches and cakes. An inexpensive source of pure protein, containing many essential vitamins and minerals, tofu makes an ideal food for those recovering from an illness, old people and children, as well as the healthy.

Chocolate

The secret of successful cooking with chocolate is to use a good quality plain chocolate, *not* one containing milk. Chocolate with milk or with a low cocoa butter content will not melt properly and will ruin your dessert. Use Cadbury's Bournville, Terry's Dark or one of the French cooking chocolates such as Chocolat Menier.

Equivalencies

I have detailed all the recipes in kilos and pounds, litres and pints. The amount in kilos and litres is not exactly the same as the amount in pounds and pints, since I have given quantities in the nearest sensible equivalent. To clarify this point: if you were living in a country where you buy vegetables in kilos, you would not buy 454 grammes (1 lb) but half a kilo (500 g). Use either metric or imperial measures throughout a recipe: do not mix them.

YOUR KITCHEN

If you are an experienced cook, then you may like to skip this section. For those of you who have recently started cooking or set up home, I list below some of the simple equipment that you will need to be a vegetarian cook, as well as some basics for your larder. So many cookery books give vast lists of expensive equipment that 'you must' have in your kitchen, but this is seldom the case and the gadgets are likely to lie unused in cupboards. My kitchen drawers are full of such 'essential' items. This basic list is adequate for even the most adventurous cook, and will save you money into the bargain!

Food processor/blender

The best investment is a food processor. This will do the work of many gadgets, is simple to use and is a real bonus for vegetarian cooking. I use mine several times a day, to purée soups, mix dips, make mayonnaise, shred vegetables, knead bread, grate cheese and much, much more. A good food processor can be bought for £50 and is an ideal wedding present, or house-warming present from a group of friends. Next best to a food processor is a blender/liquidiser. This is not normally as powerful as a food processor or as versatile but is wonderful for soups, dips and making sauces.

Saucepans

You do not need to spend a lot of money on saucepans. I buy one good saucepan at every Harrods sale (lots of department stores have wonderful kitchen reductions), which are catering seconds. Normally the reason they are seconds has little to do with the quality of the saucepan. There are fashions in saucepans as in clothes: if you buy last year's style or colour, you can often get a bargain. I bought one large casserole, very sturdy and ideal for soups, for £5 in a market. It was in an 'unfashionable' colour and I have been using it non-stop for five years.

It is a sensible investment to buy good saucepans, for they really will last. A good saucepan should be quite heavy with a strong base. Make sure the lid fits snugly; if not don't buy the saucepan. I always buy thick stainless steel with a copper bottom and a tight-fitting lid, and strong side handles. Some bargains are not worth buying. Do avoid enamel and aluminium. Enamel is not suitable for heavy cooking, only for dishes that need steaming or boiling. Aluminium saucepans can be dangerous and will not last very long.

You do not need more than four saucepans: two medium, one large and one very large. You will also need an omelette pan. Never buy very small saucepans, since they are uneconomical and a waste of money. Even if you are cooking for one, use a medium-sized saucepan. The very large (2½–3 litres/4–5 pints) saucepan is essential if you intend to make a lot of soup. It should be strong, with a heavy base: soup pans do need to be tough. Don't buy non-stick which are not suitable for soups.

A word of caution: unless you are very strong, think carefully before buying those famous, beautiful French saucepans. They are very heavy and difficult to lift even when empty. Full of water and a few pounds of vegetables, it is impossible to move them. I won't bore you with the story of what happened to my toe when the lid of one fell on it, or when I managed to spill boiling soup over my arm . . . just be warned, they look lovely but seek the opinion of friends who have them before buying!

Knives

Do not let anyone convince you that you need twenty different knives to be a good cook. Believe me, I have twenty and use only three regularly. One is a very sharp, stainless steel, French knife (which I bought very cheaply in a set from the Argos catalogue), which I use for cutting vegetables, peeling and cutting fruit. Another similar knife serves the same purposes. They have straight, long blades, are quite small (15 cm/6 in) and comfortable to use. The third knife is stainless steel with a serrated edge for cutting bread and other larger items. I store the knives in a wooden block (which you will find in department stores or mail order catalogues) made specifically for this purpose. They then can be kept sharp and you will not cut your hand reaching into a drawer.

Cutting boards

I have three wooden cutting boards that I use regularly. One is enormous, with a runnel around the rim, which serves to trap any escaping bits of food or liquid. It can be used for large quantities of salad and stores easily in a corner of the kitchen. It also doubles as a good bread board. The other two are small cutting boards, useful for small quantities. You should try to keep one for garlic and onions but I never remember. When buying a board, do lift it to test its weight. I once bought a beautiful, large, wooden vegetable board which was lovely to look at, but was very heavy and awkward to hold. I seldom used it.

Instead of one of the wooden boards, you might like to buy a plastic-coated board, which has the merit of being simple to clean as well as cheap to buy. It should be thrown out and replaced as soon as the plastic starts to peel.

Other useful items

Any vegetarian cook will need wooden spoons and a spatula. I always have at least three or four wooden spoons so that if I'm cooking different dishes, I can have one for each saucepan.

A lemon squeezer (which can be used for oranges too) is handy. I have a round, old-fashioned plastic lemon squeezer that I find much easier to use than the more modern hand presses. You can also find attractive, and effective, ones made of glass.

Many cooks find a garlic press essential. I find them such a nuisance to clean that I just use a knife and then a fork to crush the garlic.

You will need two mixing bowls, one medium-sized sieve and a large colander, a pastry brush, a grater, a small masher, a rolling pin, some baking trays and some ovenproof dishes. You may like a whisk (though your food processor may provide this function). I love those Portuguese earthenware dishes that can be found everywhere. I have them in all shapes and sizes. They are cheap, hardwearing and go from oven to freezer to oven. They also look very attractive for the table. You do need a few of them (or something similar) in different shapes and sizes, with at least one suitable for quiches and one for soufflé-type dishes.

YOUR LARDER

I like to have a basic stock of certain key items in my larder, fridge and freezer. This enables me to be able to cook a meal at any time effortlessly. I also like to buy and freeze certain seasonal items when I see them, especially if they are difficult to find. I have stopped buying in bulk – I found it to be a false economy as we couldn't consume the food while it was still fresh! I only like to keep about 2 kilos (4 lb) each of essential pulses and grains which I store in airtight glass jars. I now keep everything in glass jars after having beautiful ceramic storage jars for many years. The labels were always coming off and I never knew what was in which one! You might find this list useful when you shop.

Store cupboard

olive oil – extra virgin and pure
white wine vinegar
shoyu sauce or tamari sauce
cucumbers, chillis, peppers (bottled)
green, black, and garlic olives
muscovado or demerara sugar
thin honey
yeast extract
nuts: pistachio, walnuts or pecans, almonds, hazelnuts
sesame and sunflower seeds
chestnuts (dried and tinned)
raisins, sultanas
plain chocolate (e.g. Cadbury's Bournville)
flour: white and wholemeal
cornflour
tahini paste (in a jar)
salt, pepper, peppercorns
mustard
filter coffee
herb teas
digestive and ginger biscuits
figs and dates (dried)

pulses and grains
barley
brown rice, wild rice
buckwheat
burghul (cracked wheat)
butter beans
split peas
chick peas (dried and tinned)
couscous
ful beans (tic beans)
haricot beans
lentils: brown, green and red

Fridge

Greek yoghourt
a small carton of single cream
eggs
Feta cheese
fresh whole Parmesan
Halumi cheese
several types of goat's cheese
other favourite cheeses
butter and/or sunflower or soya spread
milk

Freezer

filo pastry
spinach
green beans
courgettes
granary, rye and wholemeal bread
pitta bread

Fresh vegetables

garlic
lettuce (iceberg)
colourful salad leaves when available
artichokes
tomatoes

potatoes
onions
cucumbers
peppers
mushrooms
leeks
aubergines
courgettes
fennel
seasonal vegetables such as swedes, parsnips and turnips
celery

Fruit

lemons
melon
avocados
kiwi fruit
passion fruit
mango
guava
oranges
apples
bananas

Herbs and Spices

Keep a stock of the following, fresh, frozen or dried
(in that order of preference)
basil
bay leaves
bouquet garni
caraway seeds
chervil
chives
cinnamon
cloves
coriander (fresh, ground and seeds)
cumin
dill
ginger
marjoram
mint

nutmeg
oregano
paprika
parsley
rosemary
tarragon
thyme
turmeric (or saffron)
vanilla pod

STARTERS

The beginning of the meal sets the tone, relaxes the diners and creates a pleasant atmosphere. I like my guests to be hungry. At dinner parties, I never offer salted nuts before the meal, just a glass of wine. I prefer not to serve too much food for the first course, and I like to vary hot and cold food. Plan your meal as a whole (I have given some suggestions in the chapter on entertaining) and vary tastes and textures. If you are serving a hot soup and a thick winter casserole, for example, serve a cold starter and finish with a cold dessert.

Many of the starters in this book can be combined to make a delicious, simple meal. In the Middle East, a large selection of different starters is often served together to form a *mezze*. Everyone dips in. Similarly, I like to invite friends for a snack-type supper mid-week when I serve lots of starter dishes, a large salad, olives and hot pitta bread. My friends arrive at nine o'clock and we spend the evening round the table, eating, drinking white wine and chatting in a relaxed and convivial atmosphere.

Remember that starters can be very simple. For unexpected visitors, simply cut up some cucumbers, tomatoes, radishes, peppers, celery (or any other combination you have in the fridge) and arrange them attractively on a plate. Add some slices of hard-boiled egg, and avocado sprinkled with lemon. Dress with a garlic mayonnaise (page 21) and serve with olives and hot pitta bread; you then have a delicious hors d'oeuvre.

The Recipes

Artichokes in Butter and Lemon Sauce
Artichoke Hearts in Garlic
Aubergine Middle Eastern Style
Avocado Dip
Avocado and Pepper Spread
Avocado Vinaigrette
Brussels Sprouts Pâté
Celeriac in Lemon Sauce
Courgettes and Mushrooms in Sour Cream
Egg and Onion
Feta and Salad
Fried Aubergine Slices
Ful Medames (Beans Egyptian Style)
Grilled Goat's Cheese
Halumi Cheese and Egg
Hummus
Leeks à la Grecque
Leeks in Tomato and Garlic Sauce
Lentil and Tahini Dip
Mushroom and Garlic Starter
Pumpkin Starter
Savoury Tomatoes
Spinach and Cream
Stuffed Mushrooms
Stuffed Onions
Tahini Dip
Turnips in Garlic and Breadcrumbs
Vegetable Antipasto with Aioli
Watercress Eggs
Winter Vegetable Hors d'Oeuvre

ARTICHOKES IN BUTTER AND LEMON SAUCE

Globe artichokes were probably brought into Britain during the reign of Henry VIII. For reasons unknown they disappeared at the end of the last century and have only become easily available very recently. They are eaten in abundance in the Middle East and the Mediterranean countries.

Artichokes are delicious and can be used as a starter or stuffed as a main course. They are also nutritious, containing iron, mineral salts and vitamins (mainly vitamin A). Choose artichokes that look green or purple. If the leaves look very dry, don't buy. Never buy tinned artichokes; they just don't taste like the real thing.

4 globe artichokes	*Sauce*
lemon juice or vinegar	200 g (8 oz) butter
	2 tablespoons lemon juice
	freshly ground pepper

Rinse the artichokes thoroughly and cut off the stalks (if these look tender, cook them with the artichokes as they may be edible). Remove any dry-looking outer leaves.

Bring to the boil a large saucepan of water. Add 2 tablespoons of lemon juice or vinegar to approximately 1 litre (2 pints) of water (this prevents the saucepan discolouring). Add the artichokes and boil for 1 hour. At this point remove one of the leaves; if it comes away easily, the artichokes are ready to eat. Remove from the heat and drain.

To make the sauce, slowly melt the butter in a saucepan. Do not allow it to brown. Add the lemon juice and a generous sprinkling of pepper.

Serve the artichokes and sauce immediately.

Note:

The edible parts of the globe artichoke are the fleshy base of the leaf and the heart; dip the base of the leaf into the sauce and chew the flesh off it. When all the leaves have been removed from the base, you are left with the artichoke heart, which is surrounded by a hairy, inedible choke. Take a knife and slowly separate the choke and heart. The heart dipped in the sauce is delicious and worth waiting for!

The butter, lemon and pepper sauce is also very good with broccoli or any other green vegetable.

ARTICHOKE HEARTS IN GARLIC

Do use fresh artichokes; tinned ones never taste like the real thing.

4 globe artichokes	4 cloves garlic
2 tablespoons fresh wholemeal breadcrumbs	200 g (8 oz) mushrooms
	olive oil
2 onions	2 teaspoons parsley, chopped

Rinse the artichokes, remove any tough outer leaves and the stalk. Boil in a large pan of water, to which you have added 2 tablespoons of vinegar or lemon juice, for 1 hour. Remove all the outer leaves. Put them in a sealed container in the fridge; you can eat them the following day with a vinaigrette sauce. Carefully remove the hairs covering the heart with a knife or a teaspoon.

Make the breadcrumbs in a food processor, or toast the bread lightly, place in a bag and crush with a rolling pin. Peel and finely chop the onions, crush the garlic and slice the mushrooms. Cook in the olive oil with the parsley for 5 minutes. Add the artichoke hearts and the breadcrumbs. Heat for an extra 2 minutes. Serve very hot with slices of granary or rye bread.

AUBERGINE MIDDLE EASTERN STYLE

Aubergine contains a very bitter juice that can spoil its taste, and it really is worth making the effort of salting and pressing the flesh to remove this juice.

I often double the quantities as this dish keeps well in the fridge for five or six days.

3 aubergines	3 tablespoons parsley, chopped
2 cloves garlic, crushed	salt
juice of 1 lemon	

Separate the flesh from the skin of the aubergines. To do this, preheat the oven to Gas Mark 4, 180°C, 375°F. Line a baking tin with silver foil, wipe the aubergines and make two holes on either side. Bake in the oven for 45 minutes, or a little longer if necessary.

Remove the skin under a cold tap and spoon the flesh into a sieve over a saucepan. Scrape all the remaining flesh off the skins. Salt very generously. Place a plate on top of the flesh and on top of that a very heavy weight (I use a saucepan full of water). Leave for at least 2 hours. Discard the black juice that collects in the saucepan.

Rinse the aubergine thoroughly to remove the salt. Mash the flesh with the crushed garlic, chopped parsley and lemon juice. Cover and leave in the fridge for an hour or so. Serve with hot pitta bread.

AUBERGINE WITH TAHINI

You can produce a variation of this dish by adding tahini to the other ingredients (see page 122, Aubergine and Tahini Spread).

AVOCADO DIP

Avocado is extremely rich in protein, vitamins and minerals, making this a highly nutritious dish. In many Mediterranean countries, babies are fed avocado and egg for their high protein. It is a very versatile food, and is also absolutely delicious!

Try to buy the black Hass variety as its taste is superior to others. To test for ripeness, gently press the flesh; it should give slightly.

This dip will keep in the fridge for two to three days.

3 medium, ripe avocado pears, skinned	2 tablespoons lemon juice
	salt and freshly ground pepper
2 hard-boiled eggs	6 tablespoons mayonnaise (see
1 large onion, finely chopped	page 22)

If you have a food processor, mix together all the ingredients and process for a few seconds only. If not, with a fork mash together the flesh of the avocados and the egg, and then add the onion, lemon juice, salt and pepper. Slowly add the mayonnaise until the mixture is fully blended; it should resemble a pâté.

Refrigerate at once in an airtight container (if the container is not fully airtight the avocado will discolour). Serve with thin slices of black, granary or rye bread.

MAYONNAISE

This mayonnaise is easy to make and keeps for a week in the fridge.

½ clove garlic	2 tablespoons white wine vinegar
2 eggs	salt and freshly ground pepper
2 tablespoons lemon juice	250 ml (½ pint) olive oil

Put the crushed garlic, eggs, lemon juice, vinegar, salt and pepper in a mixing bowl (or food processor/blender). Mix well until smooth. Slowly, drop by drop, add the oil and mix gently until the mayonnaise thickens.

This is very easy to make in a food processor or blender, slightly harder and slower by hand. If the mixture curdles, break an egg into a clean bowl, beat it, and stir in the curdled mixture firmly drop by drop.

Classic Mayonnaise is made with the egg yolks only and will produce a thicker mayonnaise. To make a classic mayonnaise, use the same recipe, but instead of 2 eggs, put in 3 egg yolks.

AVOCADO AND PEPPER SPREAD

This starter makes an unusual opening to a meal. It is also wonderful to serve as a dip at parties with small pieces of pitta bread or platters of different-coloured fresh peppers, pickled peppers, cucumber and celery. You can pickle the peppers yourself, but I normally buy them. Use the bottled version, rather than tinned, as their flavour is far superior. I usually serve this in small ramekins, but it also looks attractive served in the avocado shells.

3 avocados	2 tablespoons olive oil
1 large onion	2 tablespoons wine vinegar
1 clove garlic	salt and freshly ground pepper
1 jar pickled peppers	3 tablespoons coriander, chopped
juice of 2 lemons	

If you intend to serve the spread in the avocado shells, cut the avocados lengthways, discard the stones and gently scoop out the flesh. Sprinkle the shells inside with lemon juice.

Finely chop the onion and the garlic. Drain the peppers and cut into thin strips. Mash the avocado flesh with the lemon juice, oil and vinegar, salt and a generous amount of pepper. Mix the onion, garlic, coriander and peppers into the avocado. Cover immediately with cling film and place in the fridge until you are ready to eat. Fill small ramekin dishes or the avocado shells with the spread and serve with hot pitta bread and marinated olives.

AVOCADO VINAIGRETTE

I use avocados a lot as I used to live in Israel where they were incredibly cheap and plentiful. Whilst pregnant with my second son, all I ate for nine months were artichokes and avocados! As they both contain essential nutrients, he and I survived . . .

Avocado is delicious as a starter to a meal with this simple vinaigrette dressing. There are many different types of avocado, I always try to buy the small black, crinkly skinned Hass variety, it has a taste far superior to the other types. Always cradle the avocado in your hand; if it gives to the touch it is ripe, if you can stick your finger into it it may be too ripe. If it is hard, you can ripen it by placing it in a sealed brown paper bag with an onion or a potato for 24 hours. There is a chemical explanation for this which I have forgotten (I am somewhat unscientific) but it really does work. You may also use a plastic bag but it works better with brown paper.

6 tablespoons olive oil	1 clove garlic, crushed
2 tablespoons white wine vinegar	salt and freshly ground black
2 tablespoons lemon juice	pepper
2 teaspoons dry mustard	2 avocado pears

Mix the olive oil, vinegar, lemon juice, mustard, garlic, salt and pepper together. I do this in a clean jam-jar with a lid. Shake thoroughly. You can make large quantities and it will keep in the fridge for up to a week.

When you are ready to eat, cut the avocados in half lengthways. Remove the stone and put a half on each plate. Spoon a generous portion of the vinaigrette into the hollow left by the removed stone. Serve with brown or granary bread.

Note:
Avocado discolours when exposed to the air unless you add lots of lemon juice to it, therefore if you are using avocado in its natural state, only cut it at the last moment.

BRUSSELS SPROUTS PÂTÉ

I invented this dish in desperation one evening when I found that the ripe avocados intended for starters were bad inside. This taught me a lesson about very ripe avocados but helped me discover this easy dish. It is almost impossible to guess the pâté's main component as the sprouts' distinctive taste is mellowed by the other ingredients. Spinach, courgettes or broccoli are all equally successful in this pâté. It can be made early in the day and kept in the fridge until required.

200 g (8 oz) Brussels sprouts	1 clove garlic
1 slice granary bread	8 tablespoons mayonnaise
1 onion	salt and freshly ground pepper

Steam the Brussels sprouts until they are soft. Drain. If you have a food processor or blender, put all the ingredients together and process for a few seconds to obtain a pâté consistency. If you are making the dish by hand, make the bread into breadcrumbs (toast lightly and put into a bag and crush with a rolling pin). Mash the Brussels sprouts, onion, garlic, mayonnaise, salt and pepper together with the breadcrumbs. Refrigerate for at least 1 hour. Serve with granary bread.

CELERIAC IN LEMON SAUCE

Celeriac, a root form of celery, has never gained much popularity in Britain and has only recently become widely available. It contains significant quantities of minerals and trace elements, as well as essential vitamins, carbohydrates and protein.

One of the reasons, I think, that celeriac is so little used is that it is very awkward to peel. I was taught this tip by a French friend. Bring a saucepan of water to the boil. Make some holes in the celeriac, and boil in the water for ten minutes. Remove and drain. Prepare a bowl of water with either the juice of a lemon or two tablespoons of vinegar (to stop the rather unattractive discolouring). Peel and cut the celeriac into slices, and place them immediately in the bowl of water. This parboiling really does make peeling easier. (I also use this method with potatoes.)

2 celeriacs	juice of 2 lemons
4 tablespoons olive oil	1 tablespoon mint, crushed
1 clove garlic, crushed	

Parboil, peel and slice the celeriac as above, rinse and drain thoroughly. Heat the olive oil and very gently fry the celeriac slices and the crushed garlic. When slightly browned, add just enough water to cover. Add the juice of 1 lemon and the crushed mint. Simmer for 20 minutes. Drain off most of the liquid and reserve. Add the juice of the second lemon to the celeriac and season lightly. Mash gently. Place in individual ramekins and pour the reserved sauce on top.

26

COURGETTES AND MUSHROOMS IN SOUR CREAM

Sour cream has a distinctive taste that really enhances certain dishes. Greek yoghourt, with the addition of one tablespoon of wine vinegar, will produce a similar flavour. Try adding other vegetables, depending on the season, such as broccoli, beans, mangetout, carrots, and experiment with different flavours.

6 large courgettes	1 tablespoon marjoram, chopped
200 g (8 oz) mushrooms	1 tablespoon thyme, chopped
2 large onions	3 tablespoons white wine
2 cloves garlic	juice of 1 lemon
olive oil	250 ml (½ pint) sour cream
1 tablespoon parsley, chopped	

Prepare the vegetables and chop into thick chunks. Crush the garlic. Heat the olive oil and very gently cook all the vegetables with the herbs and garlic until softened. Add the white wine and the lemon juice and then the sour cream. Mix well. Cover the saucepan and simmer for 15 minutes. Serve very hot in little dishes with hot pitta bread.

EGG AND ONION

This is a Jewish delicacy, which is customarily eaten with the Friday night Sabbath meal. It is very simple to make and can be prepared in advance. It keeps in a fridge for two days.

3 hard-boiled eggs	4 tablespoons mayonnaise
2 onions, chopped	salt and freshly ground pepper

Mash the eggs, onions, and mayonnaise together until they form a pâté-type texture. Add salt and pepper to taste. If you normally use a food processor, only process the ingredients for a few seconds otherwise the mixture will become liquid. Chill. Serve with rye or black bread.

FETA AND SALAD

An attractive and easy starter, common in the Middle East. I use Feta cheese a lot in cooking, as it's very versatile, delicious on its own and excellent in cooked dishes.

Choose an eye-catching salad base, such as radicchio and one of the more unusual green and red salad leaves such as lollo rosso. If these aren't available, iceberg lettuce is just as good.

3 tablespoons olive oil	pinch of salt
1 tablespoon white wine vinegar	8 mixed salad leaves
1 teaspoon mustard	500 g (1 lb) Feta cheese
juice of 2 lemons	paprika
freshly ground pepper	

Mix the olive oil, wine vinegar, mustard, 1 tablespoon lemon juice, pepper and a pinch of salt (Feta cheese is very salty) to make a dressing for the salad. Dress the salad leaves and then arrange two leaves on each plate.

Line a grill-pan with silver foil and cut the Feta cheese into long, thin slices. Place under a preheated grill, turning slowly until the Feta begins to melt. Arrange on top of the salad leaves at once. Sprinkle with lemon juice and paprika.

Serve with olives (preferably the marinated garlic ones) and hot pitta bread.

FRIED AUBERGINE SLICES

I had never eaten an aubergine (or eggplant as it's called in North America and many other English-speaking countries) until I went to live in Israel. I soon made up for this lack in my culinary education as aubergines are found in great abundance in all the Middle Eastern and Mediterranean countries. Try to buy aubergines that have a slight shine to the skins. If they are shrivelled, don't buy them.

It is very important to salt and press the aubergines to remove the bitter juices. Many cookbooks claim that it is not necessary but it really does make an incredible difference.

This recipe is one of my favourites. It can also be eaten cold and will keep in an airtight container in the fridge for three or four days.

3 large aubergines	juice of 3 lemons
olive oil	4 tablespoons parsley, chopped
4 cloves garlic, crushed	salt and freshly ground pepper

Wipe the skins of the aubergines and cut lengthways into long, thick slices. Place in a sieve and salt very generously. Put the sieve over a saucepan and press the aubergine with a heavy weight (I use a saucepan containing water). Leave for at least 2 hours. Discard the bitter juices that have collected in the saucepan and rinse the aubergine very carefully to remove the salt. Dry thoroughly.

Heat the olive oil and fry the aubergine slices, turning once, and the crushed garlic until they turn a golden brown. Be generous with the olive oil, as the aubergine must be very moist. Drain on kitchen paper, and arrange in a serving dish. Sprinkle with lemon juice, chopped parsley, salt and pepper and eat with hot pitta bread.

In many Middle Eastern countries, a dressing of yoghourt and some chopped fresh mint is served with this dish.

FUL MEDAMES
(Beans Egyptian Style)

This is an Egyptian dish which is eaten all over the Middle East. When I was living in Jerusalem, I often used to eat at a very cheap restaurant where this was one of the house specialities. Served with extra tahini (sesame seed) dip (page 45), a hamin egg (an egg which has been cooked for six hours) and hot pitta bread, it was a filling and delicious meal. I buy the beans at a local Greek Cypriot grocer's shop, where they are labelled DRIED FUL (Tic bean). I have also seen them in supermarkets (with the dried pulses).

The cooked beans can be kept in an airtight jar in the fridge for five or six days.

500 g (1 lb) ful beans	2 tablespoons lemon juice
3 cloves garlic	2 tablespoons tahini dip (page 45)
olive oil	salt and freshly ground pepper
2 tablespoons parsley, chopped	

Soak the beans overnight. Boil rapidly for 15 minutes, then simmer for 2½ hours. Sieve and allow to drain. Crush in the garlic gently. Pour over 2 tablespoons olive oil, parsley, lemon juice, 2 tablespoons tahini dip, salt and pepper. Serve with hot pitta bread, and extra tahini dip on the side.

HAMIN EGGS

It is traditional to eat hamin eggs with ful medames. They are simple to make and the slow cooking produces a very delicate, creamy taste.

---

6 eggs
1 large onion

1 tablespoon real ground coffee

Place the eggs in a large saucepan, add the peeled, whole onion and lots of cold water. Add a tiny drop of oil to stop the eggs sticking. Pour the coffee into the water (this gives the eggs a wonderful colour). Cover the pan, bring to the boil and simmer for a minimum of 6 hours. Check occasionally to make sure there is still plenty of water and add more if necessary. These will keep for several days in the fridge. Serve cold with hot pitta bread, salad, and a selection of starters, such as hummus, tahini, aubergine slices, olives and ful medames, for a delicious supper meal.

GRILLED GOAT'S CHEESE

I first started eating goat's cheese when I found my body couldn't tolerate too much cow's milk, and am now an enthusiastic convert. Both goat's and ewe's cheese are very good substitutes for cow's milk cheese.

In Mediterranean countries, it is common to serve marinated goat's cheese grilled as a starter. There are many different types of goat's cheeses available (including some wonderful English and Welsh ones) so do try several!

6 small goat's cheeses (or cut large cheese into individual portions)	2 teaspoons rosemary, chopped olive oil
2 cloves garlic	1 teaspoon peppercorns
2 chilli peppers (preferably one green, one red)	2 tablespoons wine vinegar salt and freshly ground pepper
2 teaspoons thyme, chopped	salad leaves

Prepare the marinade several hours beforehand: I normally make it in the morning and leave it in the fridge all day. Put the goat's cheese in a lidded glass jar. Add the peeled but whole garlic cloves, the peppers and the thyme and rosemary. It is also customary to add a bay leaf or two, but I don't like the taste so I omit them. Pour over enough olive oil to cover totally the cheeses and peppers. Add the peppercorns. Close the jar tightly.

When you are ready to eat, cover the grill-pan with silver foil. Mix some of the marinated olive oil with the vinegar, salt and pepper to make a dressing for the salad. Arrange the salad leaves on a serving dish and pour over the dressing. Remove the cheeses from the marinade and grill until they are bubbling, then place carefully on the leaves. Serve with black bread and more salad. I like to eat the chilli peppers, too. If you haven't eaten them before, try just a little bit at first as they are STRONG . . .

The marinated cheese is delicious, too, eaten without being cooked, but in this case it needs to be left in the marinade for several days, preferably a week, before eating.

HALUMI CHEESE AND EGG

I first ate this dish in Cyprus, and always associate it with that beautiful island. Halumi cheese is now widely available in super-markets. It tastes delicious grilled or fried.

olive oil	4 eggs
500 g (1 lb) halumi cheese (cut into 4 thick slices)	lemon juice
	salt and freshly ground pepper

Heat the oil in a large frying pan. Add the cheese slices, making sure they don't touch. Cook gently and when the cheese is nearly melted, break an egg over each slice. Continue cooking until the eggs are set and sprinkle generously with lemon juice, salt and pepper. Serve with hot pitta bread. I also like to include with this dish garlic olives, which you can buy in Greek shops and some-times in supermarkets.

HUMMUS

Hummus, a Middle Eastern dish, is high in essential mineral and vitamin content and is therefore often given to children as a first food. It keeps well in the fridge for a few days, so you can make a larger quantity if you wish. It does not freeze well.

1 kilo (2 lb) chick peas	olive oil
4 tablespoons tahini	salt and freshly ground pepper
juice of 1 lemon	paprika
1 clove garlic	

Soak the chick peas in cold water overnight. Drain, add fresh water, then boil rapidly for 10 minutes and simmer for 1 hour. Drain thoroughly. If you have a food processor or blender, mix together all the ingredients. If you are making this by hand, mash the chick peas and slowly add the other ingredients.

When the mixture reaches a pâté-type consistency, slowly add a little cold water to thin slightly. The finished dish should not be too thick. Taste and add additional lemon juice if required. Allow to cool and serve with hot pitta bread. For an attractive finish, sprinkle with a little paprika and finely chopped parsley.

Note:
If you need to make this dish at short notice, tinned chick peas may be used. Drain and soak them for 15 minutes in a bowl of boiling water to remove the tinny taste.

LEEKS À LA GRECQUE

Although leeks are one of my favourite vegetables, I had never tried them cold until I was served this dish in France some years ago. I've since made it many times, as it's easy to make, can be prepared in advance and makes a tasty start to a meal. It's equally good as a vegetable accompaniment to a main dish. For a change, substitute other vegetables for the leeks: I recommend courgettes, onions, mushrooms, mangetout or carrots.

6 leeks	2 tablespoons white wine vinegar
2 garlic cloves, chopped	1 tablespoon thyme
2 wine glasses dry white wine	salt and freshly ground pepper
juice of 1 lemon	

Remove the root and any tough outer leaves then cut the leeks lengthways, and stand in a mug of boiling water for 10 minutes to remove grit. Rinse under the cold tap. Cut the leeks into 4 cm (1½ in) pieces and sauté with the chopped garlic for a few minutes on a very low heat. Add the wine, lemon juice, vinegar, thyme, salt and pepper. Simmer for 15 minutes. Allow to cool, then put in the fridge for several hours, and serve with thin wedges of granary bread. (It can also be served hot – delicious and quite different.)

LEEKS IN TOMATO AND GARLIC SAUCE

This is an excellent way to prepare leeks which I serve either as an hors d'oeuvre at a dinner party or as an accompanying vegetable dish. It can be kept for several days in the fridge in an airtight container.

750 g (1½ lb) leeks	1 onion
olive oil	2 tablespoons parsley or coriander
4 large tomatoes	salt and freshly ground pepper
3 cloves garlic	juice of 1 lemon

Cut the leeks into 10 cm (4 in) lengths and stand in a mug of boiling water for 10 minutes to loosen the grit. Rinse well under the cold tap. Heat a generous amount of olive oil in a saucepan. Add the drained leeks and simmer for 5 minutes. Turn them once. If they seem dry, add more olive oil. Chop the tomatoes, garlic, onion and parsley or coriander. Add to the leeks and continue to cook for another 10–15 minutes on a very low heat until the vegetables are tender. Add salt and pepper and the lemon juice. Eat hot or cold.

LENTIL AND TAHINI DIP

I was taught this recipe by a Persian (Iranian) neighbour, a gifted cook who used to prepare complete meals using the same vegetable throughout, yet each dish emerged with a totally different flavour. This dip will keep for a few days in the fridge if it is stored in an airtight container.

200 g (8 oz) brown lentils	4 tablespoons lemon juice
½ clove garlic, cut in two	salt and freshly ground pepper
1 onion	2 tablespoons parsley, chopped
4 tablespoons tahini	paprika

Soak the lentils for a few hours, preferably overnight. Drain and wash thoroughly. In a saucepan, cover the lentils with water, add 1 piece of garlic and the peeled onion. Bring to the boil and boil rapidly for 10 minutes. Cover the pan and simmer for 45 minutes.

In the meantime, crush the remaining garlic and mix it with the tahini paste, 2 tablespoons lemon juice, salt and pepper. This should form a thick cream; if it is very stiff, add a few drops of cold water. When the lentils are cooked, drain, and purée them with the cooked onion and garlic in a food processor/blender adding the remaining lemon juice and a tablespoon of parsley. Transfer to a serving dish and sprinkle with the remaining parsley and paprika and add a little more tahini in the centre. Eat with hot pitta bread and olives.

MUSHROOM AND GARLIC STARTER

500 g (1 lb) small mushrooms
olive oil
1 onion, cut into half rings
1 teaspoon marjoram, chopped
1 teaspoon thyme, chopped

3 cloves garlic, crushed
3 tablespoons coriander or
　parsley, chopped
1½ wine glasses dry white wine
2 tablespoons lemon juice

Wipe the mushrooms clean. Cut into chunky, bite-sized slices, or leave whole if very small. Sauté in olive oil with the onion, the marjoram, thyme and the crushed garlic. Cook very gently for 5 minutes, lower the heat and add the coriander or parsley. Continue cooking for a further 2 minutes. Add the wine, cover the pan and leave to cook for 5 minutes.

This dish can be served hot or cold. If you are eating it hot, add the lemon juice to the mixture as you serve it. It gives a very sharp taste which enhances the flavour. If you are eating it cold, allow to cool, add the lemon juice and leave in the fridge for a few hours. Serve with black bread or pitta bread.

PUMPKIN STARTER

This recipe can be made with any variety of pumpkin available. I have made it with the acorn squash, the butternut and the Turk's Turban, all successfully. For a special occasion, choose small pumpkins and serve it in the pumpkin shells, which looks very pretty and is very successful at firework-type parties.

1 pumpkin (or winter squash)	2 tablespoons orange juice
(4 oz) 100 g butter	4 tablespoons single cream or
2 tablespoons brown sugar	yoghourt
(preferably muscovado)	1 teaspoon cinnamon

Cut the pumpkin in two and place on a baking dish. Bake in a medium oven (Gas Mark 4, 180°C, 350°F) for 40 minutes. Scoop out all the flesh from the pumpkin. Place in a bowl and mash with all the other ingredients. Serve hot, either in the shells or individual ramekins, with small pieces of granary bread.

Note:
If you find this version too sweet, add a chopped onion and omit the sugar.

SAVOURY TOMATOES

This recipe can be made in advance and kept in the fridge until you need it. It is a good supper dish, and, served with hummus and pitta bread, rice and salad, makes a tasty meal. If new potatoes are available, serve them as an accompaniment with butter and parsley.

6 large firm tomatoes	4 tablespoons parsley, chopped
olive oil	½ tablespoon mustard
2 tablespoons onion, finely chopped	1 tablespoon lemon juice
2 cloves garlic, crushed	salt and freshly ground pepper

If the tomatoes are very hard, sprinkle generously with salt, leave for 1 hour and wash off salt. Scoop out the inside of the tomatoes. If this is difficult, cut the tomatoes in half and then carefully remove most of the flesh, taking care not to break the skins.

In a saucepan gently heat the olive oil and sauté the onion, garlic and parsley for a couple of minutes. Remove from the heat, add the tomato flesh, mustard, lemon juice and seasoning. Pile the mixture into the tomato skins and bake in a preheated oven at Gas Mark 4, 180°C, 350°F for 20–30 minutes.

SPINACH AND CREAM

Do try this even if you're not very keen on spinach as this recipe transforms it into a truly delicious dish.

1 kilo (2 lb) spinach	olive oil
3 onions	salt and freshly ground pepper
2 cloves garlic	3 tablespoons single cream

Wash the spinach thoroughly. Drain and then place in a large covered saucepan. Simmer for 10–15 minutes. The drops of water on the leaves will provide the necessary liquid. Drain thoroughly for 10 minutes, or wring in your hands to remove excess water.

Chop the onions and garlic and sauté in the olive oil. Drain. Place in a blender/food processor with the spinach (or mash by hand), adding lots of salt and pepper. When combined, stir in the cream.

Chill for a minimum of two hours. I like to serve this dish in individual ramekins, with granary or rye bread.

STUFFED MUSHROOMS

16 large open mushrooms
1 onion
3 cloves garlic
olive oil
½ tablespoon marjoram, chopped
½ tablespoon oregano, chopped

1 tablespoon thyme, chopped
salt and freshly ground pepper
2 slices wholemeal bread made
  into breadcrumbs
100 g (4 oz) fresh Parmesan

Wipe the mushrooms with kitchen paper. Remove the stems. Chop the stems, onion and garlic. Sauté in the olive oil and add the herbs, salt and pepper. Turn into a bowl and mix with the breadcrumbs.

In the same pan, very gently sauté the mushrooms for 2 minutes only. Place them in a greased baking dish and stuff each mushroom tightly with the breadcrumb mixture. Cover the dish. Bake at Gas Mark 4, 180°C, 350°F, for 20 minutes. Sprinkle the cheese over the mushrooms and replace in the oven, uncovered, for another 15 minutes until brown. Serve very hot.

STUFFED ONIONS

I normally make double or treble the quantity of this dish as it is rather fiddly but very worth while. It freezes well. It is good as a starter, but can also make an excellent supper dish served with a salad and a thick soup.

2 tomatoes	paprika
4 large onions	salt and freshly ground pepper
1 teaspoon parsley	1 egg, beaten
1 clove garlic	4 tablespoons olive oil
1 slice bread (preferably granary)	6 tablespoons cold water
50 g (2 oz) chopped almonds	

Stand the tomatoes in boiling water for five minutes. Remove the skin. Peel the onions and boil upright in a saucepan until they are just soft. Cut a hole in the top of each onion and very carefully remove the inside layers, leaving the outer shell intact. Chop the removed onion finely.

Chop the tomatoes, parsley and garlic. Toast the bread and crush into breadcrumbs. Mix together the chopped tomato, parsley and garlic with the breadcrumbs, nuts, a pinch of paprika, salt, pepper and the beaten egg. Stuff this mixture into each onion shell and place in a greased oven dish. Mix the olive oil and water and sprinkle over the onions to prevent them becoming too dry, cover and bake for 20 minutes in a medium-hot oven, Gas Mark 4, 180°C, 350°F.

TAHINI DIP

Tahina/tahini (both names are used, one is the Middle Eastern, one Greek) is an acquired taste; you might not like it the first time you try it, but persevere! Buy it in a jar rather than a tin. This dip keeps for several days in the fridge if stored in an airtight container.

250 ml (½ pint) tahini	salt and freshly ground pepper
3 cloves garlic, crushed	paprika
juice of 2 lemons	olive oil

If you have a food processor or blender, this only takes seconds. Blend the paste and garlic together. Slowly add the lemon juice, mixing well until a thick paste is formed. Add salt and pepper. If the mixture is very thick (it should resemble a thick cream) slowly add drops of cold water. Add extra lemon to taste.

Just before serving, sprinkle a little ground paprika and pour a trickle of olive oil over the tahini. Serve with garlic olives, hot pitta bread and, if you like them, chillies.

TURNIPS IN GARLIC AND BREADCRUMBS

A French-inspired way of cooking turnips, which also works well with parsnips and swedes. It makes an appetising starter or can be served as an accompanying vegetable.

500 g (1 lb) turnips	1 glass white wine
1 large onion	2 tablespoons brown breadcrumbs
3 cloves garlic	2 tablespoons parsley, chopped
olive oil	

Peel the turnips and onion. Cut into thin slices. Crush the garlic. Heat the olive oil and gently cook the turnips, onion and garlic for 10 minutes. Add the white wine and simmer very gently for another 10 minutes. Stir in the breadcrumbs and parsley and cook for a further minute to heat through. Serve very hot.

VEGETABLE ANTIPASTO WITH AIOLI

This antipasto is fun to eat, with each person dipping vegetables into the aioli, and can be made at different times of the year with vegetables in season. Use only fresh vegetables, not yesterday's cooked leftovers. Tasty additions are avocado purée, cauliflower florets, cooked haricot beans, broad beans or chick peas, a hard-boiled egg, olives and pickled cucumbers. The aioli can be made in a food processor or by hand.

4 courgettes	*Aioli*
200 g (8 oz) green beans	3 cloves garlic
4 leeks	juice of 1 lemon
4 broccoli sprigs	yolks of 3 eggs
12 mushrooms	salt and freshly ground pepper
olive oil	½ litre (1 pint) olive oil
8 carrots	
4 celery stalks	
1 large cucumber	
2 green, red or yellow peppers	

Salt the courgettes for 30 minutes to soften, then wash off salt and cut into long strips (they can then be gently sautéd in olive oil for a few minutes until lightly cooked, if you are not keen on raw courgettes).

Meanwhile, prepare the other vegetables. Steam the green beans, leeks and broccoli separately over a pan of boiling water for 5 minutes. Drain. Gently cook the mushrooms in olive oil for a few minutes. Slice the carrots, celery, cucumber and peppers into long strips.

Arrange the ingredients attractively on a large serving dish or individual plates, making the most of their colour combinations. Leave a space in the centre for the bowl of aioli. Keep in the fridge until 30 minutes before serving.

To make the aioli, crush the garlic, add the lemon juice, egg yolks, salt and pepper, stirring constantly. Slowly add the oil, drop by drop, until the mixture thickens, then you can add it slightly faster, in a thin trickle. If the mixture curdles, take a clean bowl, put in another egg yolk and slowly add the curdled mixture, and combine until all trace of curdling has vanished.

Serve the aioli in a small bowl in the centre of the vegetables.

Note:
If you are making large quantities for a party, you can prepare the vegetables earlier in the day and store them in the fridge in an airtight container. They will become slightly soft so make sure they are well drained first. Serve on trays with hummus, tahini, aioli, pitta bread and lots of olives.

In the Middle East, a garlic sauce is often served instead of aioli.

GARLIC SAUCE

---

4 slices of white bread, crusts removed	approx 125 ml (¼ pint) olive oil
6 cloves garlic	juice of 1 lemon
100 g (4 oz) ground almonds	salt

Crumb the bread and soak in hot water for 5 minutes, then drain by squeezing in your hand. Crush the garlic and mix into the breadcrumbs. Add the almonds and, drop by drop, slowly add the olive oil until the mixture thickens. Then add the lemon juice. The mixture will now look like mayonnaise. Add salt to taste, and possibly more lemon juice if needed.

WATERCRESS EGGS

This starter looks very pretty, and has a delicate flavour. You can prepare the eggs and the mayonnaise in advance, but do not assemble until you are ready to eat.

200 g (8 oz) watercress	salt and freshly ground pepper
6 eggs, 2 of them separated	125 ml (¼ pint) olive oil
2 tablespoons wine vinegar	

Put aside a few watercress leaves for garnish. Pour boiling water over the rest of the watercress and leave to stand for 5 minutes. Drain thoroughly. Place the watercress together with 2 egg yolks in a food processor/blender. Add the vinegar, salt and pepper. Very slowly, add the olive oil (exactly as you would to make a mayonnaise, drop by drop). The sauce will eventually thicken.

Boil the remaining eggs for 6 minutes. Cut in half, arrange cut side down and spoon the mayonnaise over. Garnish with the reserved watercress leaves.

WINTER VEGETABLE HORS D'OEUVRE

This is my contribution to nouvelle cuisine! I was served a similar dish in a French restaurant which I enjoyed so much that I came up with my own version. It's light to digest, so an ideal starter if the meal is fairly substantial, and looks very colourful. It also makes an unusual dip for a party, with strips of cucumber, peppers, celery and carrots.

---

3 large parsnips	1 large onion
200 g (8 oz) broccoli or courgettes or cauliflower, chopped	½ clove garlic, crushed
	2 tablespoons lemon juice
50 g (2 oz) butter or margarine	2 avocado pears
salt and freshly ground pepper	olives
3 tablespoons mayonnaise	

Peel and chop the parsnips. Bring to the boil in a pan of cold water, then simmer until soft. In a different saucepan, boil and simmer the chosen broccoli, courgettes or cauliflower vegetable until soft. Purée the parsnips with the butter, salt and lots of pepper in a food processor/blender, or mash by hand. Ensure that the purée is very smooth. Allow to cool. Next, purée the broccoli, courgettes or cauliflower with 1 tablespoon of the mayonnaise, half the onion, the crushed garlic, and lots of salt and pepper. Allow to cool. Mix the remaining onion, mayonnaise, lemon juice, salt and pepper with the flesh of the avocados. Arrange a little of each purée on individual plates, decorate with olives and serve with hot pitta bread.

Note:
This dish can be prepared in advance, and stored in the fridge. Keep the purées separate and cover them tightly, particularly the avocado. If you do prepare it in advance, do not place the purées on the plates until you are ready to eat.

SOUPS

There is nothing better on a cold, wintry day than a home-made soup. Fresh vegetables make marvellous soups which, served with some salad and good crusty bread, make a meal in themselves.

The ingredients

The ingredients are, of course, the most important factor. *Never* use anything that is not fresh. Soups are not dustbins for last week's old potatoes, carrots, onions, bits of cooked vegetables and de-frosted peas. If you use fresh vegetables you will always produce a good soup.

Don't use stock cubes as they will spoil the flavour of the soup. I always use yeast extract (such as Marmite) or pure soya sauce (shoyu or tamari). It is worth making the effort to find natural soya sauce (in health food shops and many supermarkets) because many of the soya brands sold in supermarkets contain vast quantities of preservatives. A tablespoon of either of these will produce an excellent stock for the vegetables. If, however, you don't like the yeast extract/soya taste, then use a vegetable stock. Next time you are making a soup, keep the skins and peelings from the vegetables. Wash them well and boil in a medium-sized saucepan with plenty of water. Boil for at least an hour, and leave to cool for several hours to allow the flavours to mingle. Taste. Use a generous tablespoon (or more) in each recipe. It can be stored for two days in the fridge in an airtight container, or frozen in ice-cube trays. I tend to avoid using very green vegetables as they dominate the stock, although you can use the stems. Choose any or all of the following: garlic, potatoes, carrots, onions, peppers, beans, peas, turnips, swedes, parsnips, mangetout, courgettes.

I prefer to use olive oil rather than butter or margarine as the taste of the olive oil definitely enhances the flavour. It is probably healthier than butter, as is suggested by the low incidence of heart disease in populations that consume vast quantities of it.

It is customary to use cream in many soup recipes. If you prefer, you can use yoghourt instead in all the recipes in this book. Greek yoghourt (particularly the variety made with sheep's milk, rather than cow's milk) works particularly well in soup. It is important that the cream or yoghourt does not boil; if it does, it will curdle.

As with any dish, herbs can transform the taste of a soup. Experiment with different herbs – tarragon, parsley, coriander, chervil, marjoram, thyme, rosemary, etc. – and you will find that the vegetables take on quite different flavours.

Soup thickeners

Many cookery books use flour as a thickener. I much prefer to thicken a soup with a potato, swede, parsnip, or turnip – ingredients that will give the same result in a far tastier way.

Time for flavours to blend

Different flavours need time to blend together. This cannot be emphasised enough in soup cookery. A soup cooked in the morning and left to stand all day will taste far better than a soup cooked and consumed immediately. A soup can also be made the evening before, cooled and stored in the fridge overnight.

To purée or not to purée

In many of the following recipes I have suggested that you purée the soup. This is purely a matter of personal preference and is not essential. If you don't like smooth soups, then eat them as they are. They will be equally delicious. Take care to cut the vegetables into smallish chunks when you are preparing. If you find the finished soup too thin or too thick for your taste, alter the water content slightly.

Freezing

All these soups freeze well. You can make double of every soup and freeze half. It takes very little extra preparation and means you have a constant supply of ready-made soups. Always freeze soup before you add cream or yoghourt, since they do not freeze well and can be added on reheating. Seasoning and herbs may need to be adjusted once the soup is defrosted as freezing diminishes their flavour.

To defrost soup, leave the frozen container in a pan for three to four hours and then slowly reheat, checking seasonings. Alternatively, defrost in the fridge overnight and then reheat. Vegetable soups will keep in the fridge for three days.

For individual portions, soup can be frozen in ice-cube trays. When the soup has frozen, turn the cubes into a plastic bag in the freezer. For adults, you need three cubes, for babies two.

Quantity

You may be surprised at the large amounts of water I have used in each recipe. I have found that it is just not worth making small quantities of soup. They need a lot of preparation and this takes the same time whether you are cooking for one or five.

You will need a large soup saucepan for the recipes in this book; I have a huge, 6-pint casserole saucepan that is excellent for soups. Soups need room to expand and you do need a saucepan that has lots of room after you have added all the water and the vegetables. Make sure the saucepan is heavy based, preferably copper based, and has handles on the side. Don't make soups in aluminium saucepans. Do read my notes on saucepans in the kitchen equipment section (page 8).

The Recipes

Avocado Soup
Barley and Vegetable Soup
Bean Soup
Broccoli Soup
Brussels Sprout and Garlic Soup
Cauliflower Soup
Celeriac Soup
Courgette and Tomato Soup
Cream of Courgette Soup
Cream of Parsnip Soup
Green or Brown Lentil Soup
Haricot Bean Soup
Jerusalem Artichoke Soup
Leek and Potato Soup
Minestrone Soup
Mushroom and Garlic Soup
Onion Soup
Pasta and Bean Soup
Pea Soup
Potato Soup
Pumpkin Cream Soup
Red Lentil Soup
Spinach Soup
Swede, Parsnip and Turnip Soup
Tomato Soup
Tomato and Onion Soup
Watercress Soup
Watercress and Wine Soup
White Bean Soup
Winter Vegetable Soup
Winter Warmer Soup

AVOCADO SOUP

This soup will mystify your visitors; no one can ever identify the avocado. It is also an acquired taste, which you will either love or hate!

1 potato, peeled and chopped	salt and freshly ground pepper
1 onion, peeled and chopped	250 ml (½ pint) single cream
2 tablespoons shoyu sauce	2 tablespoons lemon juice
3 avocados	1 wine glass vermouth
2 tablespoons coriander, chopped	

Boil the potato, onion and shoyu sauce in 1 litre (2 pints) of water for 20 minutes. Leave to cool and then purée with the avocado flesh, most of the coriander, salt and pepper. Return to the saucepan and very slowly heat as you add the cream. Do not allow the soup to boil. Remove from the heat. Stir in the lemon juice and the vermouth. Sprinkle the reserved coriander on top and serve immediately.

BARLEY AND VEGETABLE SOUP

This Eastern European soup has become very much associated with Jewish cooking and is to be found on most Jewish restaurant menus. It is very filling so prepare something light to follow.

4 carrots	olive oil
2 stalks celery	150 g (6 oz) barley
2 leeks	1 tablespoon parsley, chopped
2 onions	1 bay leaf
2 large potatoes	2 tablespoons yeast extract
250 g (8 oz) mushrooms	salt and freshly ground pepper

Chop the carrots, celery and leeks into thick slices and wash thoroughly. Peel and chop the onions and potatoes, wipe the mushrooms and slice. Heat some olive oil in a large, heavy saucepan. Gently sauté all the vegetables until they are soft. Add 2 litres (4 pints) of water, the barley, parsley, bay leaf, yeast extract and salt and pepper. Bring to the boil and then simmer, covered, for 1½ hours. Remove the bay leaf before serving. Try to leave the soup to stand for several hours.

BEAN SOUP

Any beans can be used in this soup, so try different varieties, such as haricot, broad, kidney, pinto, soya or butter. They must be properly soaked overnight and then boiled as otherwise they will cause terrible digestive problems!

This soup is very filling and makes an excellent supper dish served with rye bread and a green salad. To complete the meal, slice a mango and guava or kiwi fruit and mix with some Greek yoghourt.

500 g (1 lb) beans	olive oil
2 onions	4 tablespoons parsley, chopped
3 courgettes	3 tablespoons yeast extract
3 carrots	salt and freshly ground pepper
2 cloves garlic	

Soak the beans overnight and then rinse carefully. Transfer to a saucepan and add 2 litres (4 pints) of water. Bring to the boil and boil for 10 minutes, then simmer for 1 hour.

Chop the vegetables into chunky slices, and slice the garlic thinly. In another saucepan, heat the olive oil and gently cook the garlic. When lightly browned, add the other vegetables and cook until just soft. Add the parsley, yeast extract, the beans and their water. Season and simmer for 45 minutes.

BROCCOLI SOUP

It is common nowadays to find Calabrese – a variety of broccoli – in supermarkets and greengrocers. It looks and tastes identical to broccoli and either can be used here. Since both can taste rather bland on their own, even if seasoned generously, I like to add a small quantity of other vegetables for extra taste and colour.

Broccoli is a good source of essential vitamins and minerals, being high in vitamins B and C (more so even than oranges), and is documented as a cure for many ailments.

500 g (1 lb) broccoli	2 tablespoons shoyu sauce
2 onions	3 tablespoons coriander, chopped
2 potatoes	1 bouquet garni
2 leeks	1 glass dry white wine (optional)
2 carrots	4 tablespoons single cream or
2 cloves garlic	yoghourt (optional)
olive oil	

Wash the broccoli thoroughly, and cut into small pieces. If the stalks look a healthy green, chop them as well. Peel and chop the onions, potatoes, leeks and carrots into chunky pieces. Crush the garlic. Gently heat some olive oil and cook all the vegetables and the garlic for 5 minutes. Add 1½ litres (3 pints) of water, the shoyu sauce, coriander and bouquet garni and simmer for 1½ hours. Serve boiling hot (remove the bouquet garni before serving or else tip the herbs in the soup).

Note:
A variation is to purée the soup once it has cooled. Reheat gently, adding 1 wine glass of dry white wine 15 minutes before serving, and 4 tablespoons of single cream or yoghourt just as you are about to serve. Do not let the soup boil.

BRUSSELS SPROUT AND GARLIC SOUP

Brussels sprouts make marvellous soups as long as you add other vegetables to dilute their rather over-dominant taste. The combination with garlic here gives an unusual and flavoursome soup. When I serve it, my guests can very seldom guess the main ingredient. As so many people have an aversion to Brussels sprouts from school dinners of yesteryear, they are often very pleasantly surprised . . .

500 g (1 lb) Brussels sprouts	1 teaspoon marjoram, chopped
2 large onions	1 teaspoon thyme, chopped
3 large potatoes	1 tablespoon shoyu sauce
1 leek	salt and freshly ground pepper
3 cloves garlic	250 ml (½ pint) single cream
olive oil	

Remove the outer leaves of the Brussels sprouts. Place the sprouts in cold water for 10 minutes to wash. Drain and chop in half. Peel and chop the onions, potatoes, and the leek into chunky slices and crush the garlic. Heat the olive oil and very gently sauté the vegetables and garlic. When they are soft, add the marjoram and thyme and cook for 1 minute. Add 2 litres (4 pints) of water, the shoyu sauce, salt and pepper. Bring to the boil and simmer for 1 hour. When cool, purée in a food processor/blender.

To serve, reheat the soup, adjust the seasonings, and, off the heat, stir in the cream thoroughly. Serve at once.

CAULIFLOWER SOUP

I have not included many cauliflower recipes in this book as they are very widely available. However, whereas most recipe books seem to include lots of cauliflower cheese-type recipes, very few have recipes for cauliflower soup. Cauliflower makes a very good soup but it can taste bland if not mixed with other vegetables. I always include potatoes as they complement it well.

1 large cauliflower	salt and freshly ground pepper
3 potatoes	1 tablespoon yeast extract
2 onions	1 wine glass dry white wine
2 carrots	(optional)
3 cloves garlic	150 ml (¼ pint) single cream or
olive oil	yoghourt
2 tablespoons parsley, chopped	

Break the cauliflower into small pieces. Peel and chop the potatoes, onions and carrots into small chunks. Crush the garlic. Heat the olive oil and gently cook the carrots, onions and garlic until they are just soft. Add the cauliflower and most of the parsley and cook for another minute.

Add 2 litres (4 pints) of water, the potatoes, salt, pepper and the yeast extract and simmer for 45 minutes. Allow to cool, then purée.

Just before serving, reheat gently with the wine (if you are using it), then add the cream. Let it warm through for 1 minute on a very low heat, taking care not to let it boil. Sprinkle the rest of the parsley over.

CELERIAC SOUP

Celeriac is very under-used in this country, which is a shame because it is an excellent accompanying vegetable (it is a root vegetable, and can be cooked as potatoes, turnips or swedes), and is also very good cooked in dishes. This simple soup takes only minutes to prepare and has a delicious, unusual taste.

2 large celeriacs	2 teaspoons parsley, chopped
2 potatoes	1 tablespoon yeast extract
2 onions	salt and freshly ground pepper
½ clove garlic	4 tablespoons orange juice
olive oil	

Peel and chop the celeriacs (boiling them whole for ten minutes can make the skin easier to remove), potatoes and onions, and crush the garlic. Heat the oil and cook the celeriac, onion, parsley and garlic very gently for a few minutes. Add 1½ litres (3 pints) of water, the yeast extract, salt and pepper. Bring to the boil and then cover tightly. Simmer for 1 hour. Allow to cool, purée, then add the orange juice. Serve hot.

COURGETTE AND TOMATO SOUP

1 large onion	olive oil
1 clove garlic	2 tablespoons basil, chopped
500 g (1 lb) courgettes	2 tablespoons yeast extract
2 large potatoes	salt and freshly ground pepper
500 g (1 lb) tomatoes	1 tablespoon single cream

Chop the onion, garlic and courgettes finely. Peel and slice the potatoes. Slice the tomatoes thickly (no need to skin them). Gently heat the olive oil and add the onion, garlic and courgettes. Cover the pan and cook gently on a very low heat. Add the basil, potatoes and tomatoes and cook for a further 5 minutes. Add 2 litres (4 pints) of water, the yeast extract, salt and pepper, and bring to the boil. Cover and simmer gently for 30 minutes. Purée the soup when cool. Reheat, and, just before serving, add the single cream.

This soup freezes very well (but don't freeze with the cream); you will need to add extra salt and pepper after you have defrosted it.

CREAM OF COURGETTE SOUP

Courgettes are a most versatile vegetable and make excellent soups. This one is very quick to make.

10 courgettes	1 tablespoon thyme, chopped
2 large potatoes	2 tablespoons shoyu sauce
2 onions	salt and freshly ground pepper
1 clove garlic	3 tablespoons single cream
olive oil	

Scrub the skin of the courgettes (do not peel) and chop into chunky slices. Peel the potatoes and onions. Crush the garlic. Gently sauté the potatoes, onions, courgettes and garlic in olive oil until lightly browned, then add the thyme and cook for a further minute. Add 1½ litres (3 pints) of water, the shoyu sauce, salt and pepper. Bring to the boil. Cover the saucepan and simmer for 30 minutes. Purée when cold. Reheat, and, just before serving, swirl in the cream for an attractive, colourful effect. You might like to try this soup unpuréed. It tastes completely different.

CREAM OF PARSNIP SOUP

Parsnips and cream make an excellent combination. This filling winter soup has a slightly sweet taste which appeals to children and adults alike.

10 large parsnips	1 teaspoon marjoram, chopped
3 potatoes	2 tablespoons yeast extract
1 clove garlic	salt and freshly ground pepper
olive oil	6 tablespoons single cream
1 teaspoon rosemary, chopped	

Peel and cut the parsnips and potatoes into small pieces and crush the garlic. Sauté the vegetables with the garlic in olive oil for a few minutes until soft. Add the rosemary and marjoram and cook for another 2 minutes. Add 2 litres (4 pints) of water, the yeast extract and salt and pepper. Bring to the boil, cover tightly, and simmer gently for 40 minutes. When the soup is cool, purée it. Reheat and, just before serving, swirl in the cream and allow to heat through for a few seconds.

GREEN OR BROWN LENTIL SOUP

Lentils are a good source of protein. Although some cookery books may tell you it is unnecessary, I prefer to soak green and brown lentils (not red lentils) for several hours; this reduces the cooking time and will also allow small pieces of grit or stones to rise to the surface.

300 g (12 oz) green or brown lentils	2 leeks
2 onions	2 cloves garlic
4 carrots	olive oil
4 sticks celery	2 tablespoons coriander (if not available, use parsley), chopped
4 tomatoes	2 tablespoons yeast extract
3 potatoes	salt and freshly ground pepper
1 parsnip	

Soak the lentils for several hours and then wash thoroughly. Peel, where necessary, and chop all the vegetables into chunky pieces and crush the garlic. Heat the olive oil and very gently cook all the vegetables with the garlic for 10 minutes, until they are just soft. Add the lentils, coriander, yeast extract, salt and pepper and 1½ litres (3 pints) of water. Bring to the boil for 10 minutes, cover the saucepan and then simmer for 1 hour.

HARICOT BEAN SOUP

A substantial cold-weather soup. Carrots give the soup more flavour and an attractive golden hue.

300 g (12 oz) haricot beans	1 bouquet garni
4 large carrots	1 bay leaf
2 onions	2 tablespoons shoyu sauce
1 clove garlic	salt and freshly ground pepper
olive oil	

Soak the beans overnight, or for a minimum of 6 hours. Rinse and drain, then boil rapidly for 15 minutes in 1 litre (2 pints) of water.

Peel and chop the carrots, onions and garlic. Sauté the onions and garlic in a little olive oil for 3 minutes. Add the carrots, 1½ litres (3 pints) of water, the bouquet garni, bay leaf and the shoyu sauce. Add the beans and the bean water. Bring to the boil and simmer, covered, for 1½ hours. Before serving, remove the bouquet garni and the bayleaf and add salt and pepper to taste.

JERUSALEM ARTICHOKE SOUP

Jerusalem artichokes are the most misnamed vegetable, being neither an artichoke nor having any association with Jerusalem. They are a knobbly root vegetable and bear no resemblance to the globe artichoke. Their name supposedly comes from the Italian *girasole* (sunflower) to which they are related. Various other theories as to the origin of the name have been suggested, none of them very conclusive. Don't serve too many at any one meal, since some people find them difficult to digest.

Jerusalem artichokes are versatile, delicious as a vegetable served with butter, or in soup, which makes the most of their unusual earthy taste.

750 g (1½ lb) Jerusalem artichokes	2 cloves garlic
2 onions	olive oil
250 g (8 oz) potatoes	3 tablespoons yeast extract
3 tablespoons parsley	salt and freshly ground pepper

Boil the Jerusalem artichokes for 15 minutes. Drain and run them under a cold water tap to remove the skins. Place in a little water containing 1 tablespoon of vinegar to prevent any discoloration. Chop the onions, potatoes and parsley, and crush the garlic. Heat the olive oil and gently cook the potatoes, onions, garlic and most of the parsley, reserving some for garnish. Drain the artichokes, chop, and add to the pan.

Cook on a very low heat until the vegetables are softened, then add 1½ litres (3 pints) of water, the yeast extract, salt and pepper. Simmer for 1 hour. Serve very hot with the remaining parsley sprinkled on top. If you prefer smooth soups this can be puréed.

LEEK AND POTATO SOUP

Leeks have been consumed for thousands of years, and their medicinal applications appear throughout history. They are mentioned in the Old Testament and were widely eaten by the Egyptians and Israelites. They have been a constant part of our diet since Saxon times, but few people nowadays seem to appreciate their versatility. They are shown at their best in this easy recipe, one of my favourite soups.

500 g (1 lb) leeks	2 onions
2 cloves garlic	2 tablespoons yeast extract
500 g (1 lb) potatoes	salt and freshly ground pepper
3 tablespoons parsley, chopped	3 tablespoons single cream or
olive oil	yoghourt

Cut the leeks in half lengthways, removing the root. Stand in a mug of boiling water for 10 minutes to remove grit and then rinse in a sieve.

Roughly chop the garlic, leeks, potatoes and parsley. Heat the olive oil. Sauté the garlic, potatoes, peeled and chopped onions and leeks very gently for a few minutes and then add the parsley. When the vegetables look slightly cooked but not brown, add 2 litres (4 pints) of water, the yeast extract, salt and pepper and bring to the boil. Simmer for 1 hour.

When cool, purée, and add extra salt and pepper to taste. To serve, reheat the soup and swirl in the cream at the last moment.

MINESTRONE SOUP

A variation of the traditional Italian soup which, served with salad and a plate of good cheeses with French bread and butter, makes a substantial supper.

150 g (6 oz) haricot beans	300 g (12 oz) tomatoes
3 onions	olive oil
3 leeks	4 tablespoons parsley, chopped
3 stalks celery	2 tablespoons basil, chopped
5 carrots	2 tablespoons oregano, chopped
4 courgettes	salt and freshly ground pepper
100 g (4 oz) runner beans	4 tablespoons yeast extract
1 green pepper	200 g (8 oz) macaroni
2 cloves garlic	

Soak the dried haricot beans overnight. Drain, then boil for 15 minutes in 500 ml (1 pint) of water. Retain the water. Peel, where necessary, and chop all the vegetables into chunky pieces.

In a very large saucepan, heat the olive oil and sauté the garlic and onions. Slowly add the leeks, carrots, runner beans, celery, courgettes and pepper and cook for 3 minutes. Add the parsley, basil and oregano. Cook for a couple of minutes more, then add the tomatoes, salt and pepper. Add 1½ litres (3 pints) of water, the yeast extract, and the haricot beans with their water. Bring gently to the boil, cover and simmer for 1 hour. Add the macaroni and boil for a few minutes. Remove from the heat and leave to stand, covered, for 20 minutes. Adjust seasoning if necessary. If you are making the soup in advance, add the macaroni 30 minutes before serving.

Reheat, and serve with a bowl of freshly grated Parmesan cheese to sprinkle over, and French bread and butter.

MUSHROOM AND GARLIC SOUP

This is a warming soup that I make often in winter, and one which benefits particularly from being prepared in advance.

2 leeks	2 tablespoons tarragon, chopped
500 g (1 lb) mushrooms	2 tablespoons shoyu sauce
4 cloves garlic	salt and freshly ground pepper
2 large courgettes	150 ml (¼ pint) single cream or
3 large onions	yoghourt
olive oil	

Slice the leeks in two lengthways and place in a mug of boiling water for 10 minutes to remove dirt. Wipe the mushrooms and chop. Crush the garlic, and chop the courgettes, leeks and onions into chunky pieces. Sauté in the olive oil for 5 minutes. Add most of the tarragon and cook for another minute. Add 1½ litres (3 pints) of water, the shoyu sauce, salt and pepper. Bring to the boil and then simmer for 1 hour.

When required, reheat the soup thoroughly, and add the cream or yoghourt, allowing it to warm but not boil. Sprinkle with the reserved tarragon.

ONION SOUP

This is a variation on the traditional French onion soup which I like to serve with croûtons and cheese. Some cooks use flour to thicken the soup but I don't like to do this as I think it spoils the taste. I always use potato which is a natural thickener and also enhances the onion flavour.

6 onions	1 tablespoon yeast extract
2 large potatoes	100 g (4 oz) Gruyère, Gouda,
2 cloves garlic	Edam or Cheddar cheese,
olive oil	grated, or other favourite
1 teaspoon marjoram, chopped	variety (optional)
1 teaspoon thyme, chopped	croûtons (optional)
salt and freshly ground pepper	

Peel and chop the onions and potatoes into thick chunks. Crush the garlic. Heat the oil and very gently cook the onions and garlic until they are lightly browned. Add the herbs and cook an extra minute. Add 2 litres (4 pints) of water, the potatoes, salt, pepper and the yeast extract. Bring to the boil then cover and simmer for 1 hour. Adjust seasoning and serve with a little of the grated cheese and croûtons in each bowl.

CROÛTONS

Take 2 slices of wholemeal bread and butter generously. Crush 1 clove of garlic and spread over the bread. Grill until just brown. Cut into small pieces and sprinkle into individual bowls of soup. If you wish to make a large quantity and freeze them, wrap the buttered garlic bread in silver foil and place in a hot oven for 15 minutes.

PASTA AND BEAN SOUP

An Italian soup which is nearly a meal in itself. I serve it as a supper dish with garlic or herb bread, a large salad and a baked potato. Any type of white bean, such as haricot, can be used, although in Italy borlotti beans are generally used in this recipe. These are widely available here in tins but only Italian grocers are likely to stock them fresh or dried. You can use any type of small pasta in the soup; I like to use thick noodles but any form of small macaroni is fine.

500 g (1 lb) white beans	6 tomatoes
2 onions	2 tablespoons parsley, chopped
1 green pepper	2 tablespoons yeast extract
3 carrots	salt and freshly ground pepper
3 sticks celery	200 g (8 oz) noodles or small
2 cloves garlic	macaroni
olive oil	freshly grated Parmesan

Soak the beans overnight. Peel, where necessary, and chop all the vegetables except the tomatoes. Heat the olive oil and cook the chopped vegetables gently until soft. Add the tomatoes and the chopped parsley and cook a further 1 minute. Don't let the mixture get dry or stick; add extra olive oil if necessary.

Add 2 litres (4 pints) of water, the yeast extract, salt and pepper. Drain and wash the beans and add to the saucepan. Boil rapidly for 15 minutes, then cover and simmer for 1 hour. Leave to stand for a few hours.

When required, check the seasoning, bring the soup to the boil, add the pasta and cook for no more than 10 minutes so that it retains its bite. Serve with a small bowl of freshly grated Parmesan on the table to be added to taste.

Note:
If you wish to freeze this soup, freeze before the pasta is added as it is inclined to taste soggy when defrosted. Add the pasta when reheating.

72

PEA SOUP

I normally use split peas for this soup, but I have also made it quite successfully with frozen peas when I've forgotten to soak the peas overnight or wanted to make a quick soup. It tastes quite different, but is nonetheless surprisingly good. This soup also tastes very good chilled.

500 g (1 lb) split peas
3 onions
2 cloves garlic
1 teaspoon parsley, chopped
olive oil

2 tablespoons shoyu sauce
salt and freshly ground pepper
4 tablespoons single cream or
   yoghourt

Soak the split peas overnight, then drain and rinse. Peel and chop the onions and garlic. Gently heat the oil, and cook the onions and garlic. When they start to soften, add the peas and parsley and cook for 1 minute. Add 1½ litres (3 pints) of water, the shoyu sauce and salt and pepper. Bring to the boil and boil for 10 minutes, then simmer for 1 hour (30 minutes if you have used fresh or frozen peas). Allow to cool slightly and purée. To serve, reheat the soup and swirl in the cream or yoghourt.

POTATO SOUP

Potato is a wonderful vegetable to use in soups, either on its own or as a natural thickener with other vegetables. This recipe makes use of extra vegetables to enhance the colour and flavour. It can be blended and mixed with cream or yoghourt to make a smooth, creamy soup, or served chunky. The taste is quite different!

750 g (1½ lbs) potatoes
2 onions
2 carrots
2 sticks celery
3 cloves garlic
olive oil

3 tablespoons coriander, chopped
2 tablespoons shoyu sauce
salt and freshly ground pepper
150 ml (¼ pint) single cream or
        yoghourt (optional)

Peel and chop the potatoes and onions into small, thin slices. Scrub the carrots and celery and chop into small pieces. Crush the garlic. Heat the olive oil, and cook the vegetables and garlic and most of the coriander for 3 minutes. Add 1½ litres (3 pints) of water, the shoyu sauce, salt and pepper. Simmer for 1 hour. When you are ready to eat, reheat and adjust the seasonings.

If you wish, blend the soup and gently reheat with the cream or yoghourt (don't let it boil). Sprinkle some chopped coriander on top for colour.

PUMPKIN CREAM SOUP

Any variety of pumpkin can be used for this prettily coloured soup, although I normally use the small orange/green Turk's Turban. It freezes very well, but freeze before you add the cream.

1 kilo (2 lb) pumpkin	1 tablespoon thyme, chopped
3 large potatoes	2 tablespoons shoyu sauce
2 onions	salt and freshly ground pepper
olive oil	4 tablespoons single cream

Cut the pumpkin in half, remove the seeds, place on a baking dish and bake in the oven (Gas Mark 4, 180°C, 350°F) for 40 minutes. Spoon out the flesh when cooked, and chop.

Peel and chop the potatoes and onions. Gently cook them in the olive oil until lightly browned. Add the flesh of the pumpkin, thyme, 1½ litres (3 pints) of water, shoyu sauce and salt and pepper. Bring to the boil, cover, and simmer for 45 minutes. Leave to cool then blend until smooth. To serve, reheat the soup and swirl in the cream. This looks very attractive.

RED LENTIL SOUP

Red lentils are full of protein and essential nutrients, do not need to be soaked and are a colourful addition to many dishes. They make a flavoursome, filling soup.

3 carrots	olive oil
2 onions	2 tablespoons parsley, chopped
1 large parsnip	300 g (12 oz) red lentils
2 large potatoes	1 ½ tablespoons yeast extract
2 cloves garlic	salt and freshly ground pepper

Peel and chop the vegetables into thick chunks. Crush the garlic. Heat the olive oil and gently cook the parsnip, onions and garlic. Add the parsley and lentils and cook until slightly browned. Add 2 litres (4 pints) of water, the potatoes, carrots, yeast extract and salt and pepper. Bring to the boil then simmer, covered, for 1 hour.

SPINACH SOUP

According to Jane Grigson, author of very informative and interesting cookery books, spinach was given by the King of Nepal to the Emperor of the T'ang Dynasty in 647. Its history goes back a long way, although it does seem to have originated in Persia. The medicinal properties of spinach are well known (most of these predate Popeye by a long way!) and range from combating anaemia, helping blood to clot and as a cure for constipation.

Like many of my generation, I wouldn't touch spinach for years until I was served it in France where it is cooked in many delicious ways. This soup is based on a recipe I learned in France at one of those wonderful little restaurants whose exterior belies the beauty of the food within.

500 g (1 lb) spinach	1 teaspoon marjoram, chopped
2 onions	1 teaspoon rosemary, chopped
2 cloves garlic	2 tablespoons yeast extract
2 potatoes	salt and freshly ground pepper
olive oil	250 ml (½ pint) single cream or
2 tablespoons parsley, chopped	yoghourt

Wash and drain the spinach thoroughly. Peel, where necessary, and chop the onions, garlic and potatoes. Heat the olive oil, and cook all the vegetables, garlic and herbs, reserving a little parsley to garnish, until they are soft. Add 1½ litres (3 pints) of water and stir in the yeast extract. Add salt and pepper and simmer for 1 hour. Leave to cool completely and purée.

Reheat the soup and slowly add all but 1 tablespoon of the cream, taking care not to let it boil. Just before serving, swirl in the tablespoon of cream to produce a pretty marbled effect, and sprinkle with the remaining parsley.

SWEDE, PARSNIP AND TURNIP SOUP

This is a very welcoming soup on a wintry day. Don't cook a huge meal after it, as it really is rich. Unfortunately, these root vegetables seem to be rather neglected in Britain, and we seldom use them imaginatively, perhaps because they have been around for so long. Parsnips and turnips have been grown in Britain since Roman times; swedes were introduced much more recently, some 200 years ago. All three vegetables are high in essential vitamins, minerals, trace elements, carbohydrate and dietary fibre. They are therefore a good food to serve to invalids or children recovering from an illness. Children often like this soup as the parsnips give it an unusual sweetness. If you don't like pale soups, add two carrots to the recipe and sprinkle with one tablespoon of chopped parsley before serving.

200 g (8 oz) swedes	olive oil
200 g (8 oz) parsnips	2 teaspoons marjoram, chopped
200 g (8 oz) turnips	2 tablespoons yeast extract
100 g (4 oz) potatoes	salt and freshly ground pepper

Peel the vegetables and cut into chunky pieces. Heat the oil and cook the vegetables for 10 minutes. Add the marjoram and cook for another minute. Add 1½ litres (3 pints) of water, the yeast extract, salt and pepper and simmer for 1½ hours. You may need to add extra water. Leave to stand for several hours, and reheat when required.

TOMATO SOUP

Tomato soup is very simple to make, and here the basil and garlic combine to give the soup a sweet taste. Use fresh tomatoes as tinned ones really don't taste the same. I like to use potato to give the soup some thickness (in Italy a slice of bread is often used for the same purpose) although this is not essential and the soup tastes equally good, albeit thinner, without it. Vary the herb each time you make this to give a slightly different taste: try coriander, chives, parsley, chervil, tarragon, marjoram or thyme. Add the vermouth for special occasions. It really gives the soup a very special flavour.

1 kilo (2 lb) tomatoes	1 tablespoon yeast extract
2 large potatoes	salt and freshly ground pepper
2 cloves garlic	250 ml (½ pint) single cream or
3 tablespoons basil, chopped	yoghourt
olive oil	1 wine glass vermouth (optional)

Wash the tomatoes and chop them (skin and all) into thick chunky slices. Peel the potatoes and crush the garlic. Chop the basil. Heat the olive oil and very gently cook the tomatoes, garlic and most of the basil for 5 minutes. Add 2 litres (4 pints) of water, the potatoes, the yeast extract and salt and pepper. Bring to the boil and then simmer for 45 minutes. Leave to stand for several hours and then purée.

When you are ready to eat, reheat the soup and gently add most of the cream or yoghourt, allowing it to heat through but not boil. Remove the saucepan from the heat and stir in the vermouth. Swirl in a drop of cream and sprinkle over the remaining basil for an attractive effect. Serve at once.

TOMATO AND ONION SOUP

This soup is a very good source of protein, and, if blended, is ideal as a first baby food. I always serve it to the family after illness, since it tastes sweet and is enjoyed by all ages.

150 g (6 oz) red lentils	1 clove garlic
3 onions	olive oil
2 carrots	2 tablespoons parsley, chopped
2 potatoes	2 tablespoons yeast extract
500 g (1 lb) tomatoes	salt and freshly ground pepper

Wash the lentils thoroughly and then drain. Prepare and chop the vegetables and crush the garlic. Heat the olive oil gently. Add the vegetables and garlic and cook for 10 minutes until they are soft. Add the lentils and parsley and cook for a minute more, adding extra olive oil if the mixture shows signs of sticking. Add 2 litres (4 pints) of water, the yeast extract and salt and pepper. Bring to the boil and then simmer for 1 hour.

WATERCRESS SOUP

The history of watercress can be traced back to very early times. It appears in many ancient texts and was considered by the Romans and Elizabethans as having special medicinal properties, being used to cure mental illness, scurvy, headaches, dermatitis, rheumatism and a long list of other ailments. It has also been recommended as an aphrodisiac, a treatment for kidney ailments and a cure for asthma. It is rich in many essential vitamins and trace minerals and a good source of calcium. Surprisingly enough, even with this long list of claims, it is also delicious!

500 g (1 lb) watercress	1 teaspoon marjoram, chopped
1 clove garlic	1 teaspoon thyme, chopped
3 large onions	salt and freshly ground pepper
olive oil	250 ml (½ pint) single cream or
500 g (1 lb) potatoes	yoghourt
2 tablespoons shoyu sauce	

Wash and chop the watercress. Peel and chop the garlic and onions. Retain some of the watercress for decoration. Heat the olive oil and add the vegetables and chopped herbs. Peel and chop the potatoes and add to the oil. Let the vegetables cook gently. Add 1½ litres (3 pints) of water and slowly bring to the boil, add the shoyu sauce, salt and pepper, then reduce the heat to a simmer. Continue to cook for 40 minutes, allow to cool and purée.

To serve, reheat gently and slowly add almost all the cream and adjust seasonings. Swirl the rest of the cream on top for an attractive effect and add the reserved watercress to garnish.

WATERCRESS AND WINE SOUP

A perfect soup for special occasions.

500 g (1 lb) potatoes	1 tablespoon tarragon, chopped
2 onions	1 tablespoon shoyu sauce
3 cloves garlic	salt and freshly ground pepper
500 g (1 lb) watercress	250 ml (½ pint) dry white wine
olive oil	250 ml (½ pint) single cream

Peel and chop the potatoes, onions and garlic. Wash and chop the watercress, retaining a small amount for decoration. Heat the olive oil and very gently cook the potatoes, onions, watercress and garlic until they are slightly soft. Add the tarragon and cook for an extra minute. Add 1½ litres (3 pints) of water, the shoyu sauce, salt and pepper and bring to the boil. Boil for 10 minutes, cover and then simmer for 45 minutes.

Purée the soup once cool. To serve, reheat gently and stir in the white wine, then the cream, taking care not to let the soup boil. Sprinkle with the reserved watercress.

WHITE BEAN SOUP

An ideal soup for those cold, long winter nights. Served with French bread, a chunky salad and baked potatoes, it makes a very satisfying supper. As it takes some time in preparation, do make large quantities. If you prefer, you can omit the vegetables but I find they add extra colour and flavour to the soup.

200 g (8 oz) haricot beans	2 cloves garlic
100 g (4 oz) butter beans	olive oil
100 g (4 oz) dried green peas	3 tomatoes
2 large potatoes	2 tablespoons tamari/shoyu sauce
1 leek	2 tablespoons parsley or
4 carrots	coriander, roughly chopped
2 onions	salt and freshly ground pepper
3 courgettes	

Soak both types of beans and peas together in cold water overnight. Drain, transfer to a saucepan and add 2 litres (4 pints) of water. Bring to the boil and boil rapidly for 15 minutes, cover, and simmer for 1 hour.

Prepare and chop all the vegetables except the tomatoes into chunky pieces. Crush the garlic. Lightly sauté in the olive oil until they are just cooked. Add the beans and peas with their water, the whole tomatoes, tamari (or shoyu) sauce, parsley or coriander and salt and pepper. Bring to the boil and then simmer for 45 minutes. Serve boiling hot.

WINTER VEGETABLE SOUP

This filling soup can be made with any combination of vegetables but do not omit the potatoes.

It is essential to make this soup several hours (or even a whole day) before you need it as the flavours of the vegetables need time to blend together. I make it in the morning and in the evening it tastes great! This recipe produces a large quantity and I freeze half; it's worth making big quantities as the vegetables take quite a while to prepare.

3 onions	1 turnip or swede
300 g (10 oz) potatoes	2 leeks
2 cloves garlic	olive oil
4 carrots	1 teaspoon marjoram, chopped
2 parsnips	1 teaspoon thyme, chopped
100 g (4 oz) mushrooms	2 teaspoons parsley, chopped
100 g (4 oz) green beans	2 teaspoons tamari sauce
6 stalks celery	salt and freshly ground pepper
2 courgettes	

Wash, peel where necessary, and chop all the vegetables into thick chunks. Heat the olive oil gently in a large saucepan and cook the vegetables until they are all translucent. Add the herbs and continue to cook for another 2 or 3 minutes. Add 2 litres (4 pints) of water, the tamari sauce and salt and pepper. Bring to the boil, cover tightly and simmer for 1 hour. Check that the vegetables are soft. If they are, switch off the heat but leave the saucepan to stand for several hours. If they do not seem sufficiently cooked, simmer for another 30 minutes. Reheat and serve piping hot. (If you prefer a smooth soup, purée it once it has cooled.)

WINTER WARMER SOUP

A dear friend, now in her seventies, was taught this recipe by her Polish Jewish grandmother. It's a classic winter soup, nearly a meal in itself. You can vary the vegetables (try turnips or swedes instead of potato).

100 g (4 oz) split peas	4 stalks celery
100 g (4 oz) butter beans	4 large potatoes
100 g (4 oz) green lentils	olive oil
100 g (4 oz) barley	1 bay leaf
8 carrots	4 tablespoons parsley, chopped
2 cloves garlic	4 tablespoons yeast extract
3 onions	salt and freshly ground pepper

Soak the split peas, butter beans and green lentils together overnight. Wash and drain. Wash the barley. Peel where necessary, and chop the carrots, garlic, onions, celery and potatoes and sauté in the oil for 3 minutes until lightly browned. This seals in the flavour and makes a big difference to the final taste. Add the washed barley, peas, beans and lentils, and then the parsley, bay leaf, 2 litres (4 pints) water mixed with the yeast extract, and salt and pepper. Bring to the boil for 15 minutes, cover and simmer for 2½ hours. Remove the bay leaf. Leave for several hours to stand. Reheat and serve very hot.

MAIN COURSES

It is very easy when preparing a meal with several courses to end up with lots of delicious food that just doesn't go together. I like to plan a meal *as a whole*, so that the main course complements the starter and dessert. I also try to plan the accompanying vegetables and salads carefully. Winter meals require particular care because some of the main courses are very filling and you do not always need starters *and* soups *and* desserts as well.

Plan, also, the different elements of the main course. Too many different vegetables make the taste of the main course disappear, so I often cook some of the vegetables I am using in the main dish and serve them with the meal. If you think you have enough vegetables (for example if your main dish is aubergine stuffed with rice and vegetables), serve a large mixed salad. Don't serve more than one 'filler' (rice, potatoes, pasta) and select one that goes with the theme of the meal (Mediterranean, Middle Eastern, etc.).

The Recipes

Baked Aubergine and Tomato
Banana and Nut Pilaf
Broccoli and Cheese Bake
Buckwheat and Vegetable Pilaf
Cashew Nut, Vegetable and Cheese Flan
Chestnut Casserole
Chick Pea Pasta
Couscous and Vegetables
Fennel Delight
Hazelnut and Vegetable Pilaf
Leeks Croustade
Lentil Hotpot
Lentils with Vegetables
Mushroom and Curd Cheese Marjoram Pie
Mushrooms in Filo Pastry
Mushroom Pilaf
Mushroom Stroganoff
Okra and Tomato Pilaf
Parsnip and Onion Soufflé
Pasta and Pepper Sauce
Pumpkin Pie
Pumpkin and Burghul Pie
Spaghetti alla Pirata
Spanakopitta (Spinach and Feta in Filo Pastry)
Stuffed Artichokes
Stuffed Aubergines (Courgettes or Peppers)
Stuffed Vine Leaves
Tofu Chinese Style with Vegetables
Vegetable Stroganoff
Winter Quiche
Winter Warmer Casserole

BAKED AUBERGINE AND TOMATO

If you are not used to cooking aubergine (or eggplant as it is called in many English-speaking countries), then do note that it contains a very bitter juice which it is important to remove, by salting and pressing, before cooking.

2 medium or 3 small aubergines	1 slice wholemeal toast for
1 large onion	breadcrumbs
500 g (½ lb) tomatoes	olive oil
100 g (4 oz) Parmesan cheese or	2 eggs, beaten
Feta cheese	salt and freshly ground pepper
2 tablespoons parsley	

Cut up the aubergines into small pieces and put into a large sieve over a saucepan, sprinkle very generously with salt and compress with a large weight (I use a saucepan full of water). Leave for at least 2 hours. The bitter juice will collect in the lower saucepan. Wash the aubergine thoroughly to remove the salt.

Skin and chop the onion, chop the tomatoes, grate or crumble the cheese and chop the parsley. Make the breadcrumbs in a food processor or toast a slice of bread, put the toast in a plastic bag, and crush with a rolling pin.

Heat the olive oil slowly in a heavy-based saucepan, and add the aubergines and onion. Cook gently for 15 minutes with the pan covered. Then stir until the mixture is lightly browned, adding extra olive oil if it sticks to the pan. Drain off any excess oil, then mix in the breadcrumbs, beaten eggs, parsley, salt and a generous amount of pepper.

Lightly grease an ovenproof dish with olive oil. Cover the base with the tomatoes (mash them gently). Add the aubergine mixture, and sprinkle the cheese on top. Cover with silver foil.

Bake in a preheated oven at Gas Mark 5, 190°C, 375°F, for 30 minutes. Remove foil and bake uncovered for a further 15 minutes. Serve with plain rice and a green salad.

Note:
As a variation, omit the eggs, and pour 2 tablespoons of olive oil over the aubergine mixture before adding the cheese. This gives quite a different texture.

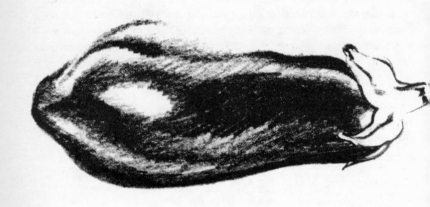

BANANA AND NUT PILAF

Some friends from abroad were delayed in arriving, were starving but felt too exhausted to go to a restaurant as planned. I therefore needed to cook something quick and easy while they were en route from the airport, knowing that they would eat any vegetarian non-dairy dish. This recipe was the result, invented at the last minute. I served it with a large salad, followed by mango and honey as dessert.

2 large onions	500 g (1 lb) long grain brown rice, washed
1 clove garlic	
100 g (4 oz) mushrooms	2 teaspoons saffron or turmeric (optional)
2 green peppers	
olive oil	salt and freshly ground pepper
100 g (4 oz) parsley or coriander, chopped	100 g (4 oz) sultanas or raisins
	3 bananas
100 g (4 oz) pine nuts (if unavailable use walnuts)	225 g (8 oz) carton yoghourt (optional)

Peel and finely chop 1 onion and crush the garlic. Chop the mushrooms and peppers. Gently sauté the onion and garlic in olive oil then add the mushrooms, parsley or coriander and peppers. Add the pine nuts when the vegetables are slightly browned. Cook for an additional minute, add the rice and gently simmer until the rice is glazed. Add twice the amount of water to the rice (I measure the rice in a mug and use the same mug to measure the water). Add the turmeric or saffron (to give the rice a yellow colour), salt and pepper and bring to the boil. Boil for 5 minutes and then cover the saucepan tightly. *Do not stir* the rice once it has boiled, or it will become starchy. Leave to simmer for 35 minutes. Lift the lid to see if the surface of the rice is pitted with little holes. If it is, replace the lid, switch off the heat but do not move the pan for at least 30 minutes (this allows the heat of the steam to dry the rice and gives it an improved flavour). If the rice still needs cooking, leave for another 15 minutes. Do not stir.

When the rice has been cooking for 15 minutes, prepare the bananas. Peel and chop them into chunks, and then slice the remaining onion into rings. Soak the raisins in boiling water for 10 minutes. Drain. Heat some olive oil and sauté the onion until golden brown, then add the bananas. Continue to cook until the bananas are golden brown and the onion has caramelised. Add a sprinkling of salt and pepper and the raisins. Serve over the hot rice. If this dish seems too dry, spoon a little yoghourt over each serving.

BROCCOLI AND CHEESE BAKE

A quick, easy dish to prepare for supper.

500 g (1 lb) broccoli (or Calabrese)	100 g (4 oz) butter or margarine
salt and freshly ground pepper	200 g (8 oz) Halumi, goat's, Feta or Parmesan cheese

Boil a large saucepan of water with a sprinkling of salt. Chop the broccoli into small florets. If the stalks look healthy, cut them into small pieces. Add to the boiling water and cook for 15 minutes. Drain. Butter an ovenproof dish and arrange the broccoli evenly in it. Add salt and pepper, dot with butter and grate the cheese over. (Vary the cheese each time for a different flavour.) Place in a preheated oven, Gas Mark 4, 180°C, 350°F, until golden brown (about 15–20 minutes). Serve at once.

BUCKWHEAT AND VEGETABLE PILAF

Buckwheat makes a good alternative to rice. It is a plant high in nutrients and can be bought either in its natural state or roasted. Here I have used the natural version.

1 green pepper	olive oil
1 clove garlic	3 tablespoons coriander, chopped
4 carrots	3 tablespoons parsley, chopped
4 courgettes	salt and freshly ground pepper
3 onions	3 tablespoons shoyu sauce
200 g (8 oz) buckwheat	

Peel, where necessary, and chop all the vegetables into chunky slices. Wash the buckwheat. Gently heat the olive oil and slowly cook the vegetables and herbs until soft. Add the buckwheat and cook for 5 minutes. Add enough water to cover, salt, pepper and the shoyu sauce. Simmer for 20 minutes. Just before serving, place in a preheated medium oven (Gas Mark 4, 180°C, 350°F) for 10 minutes.

CASHEW NUT, VEGETABLE AND CHEESE FLAN

The rather unusual blend of flavours here make a delectable flan. Try substituting different cheeses, such as Feta or Cheddar, in place of the Parmesan.

Pastry
150 g (6 oz) flour
75 g (3 oz) margarine
cold water
pinch of salt

Filling
2 onions
4 courgettes
4 leeks

1 clove garlic
olive oil
5 tablespoons coriander, chopped
100 g (4 oz) cashew nuts
3 eggs
4 tablespoons milk
100 g (4 oz) Parmesan cheese,
    freshly grated
salt and freshly ground pepper

First of all, make the pastry. Add the salt to the flour and rub the flour and margarine together to form crumbs. Add cold water (start with 2 tablespoons, and add 1 more if this is not enough) and knead into a dough. Wrap in foil and rest in the fridge until you have prepared the filling. (Pastry is much easier to handle when it is chilled.)

Prepare all the vegetables and chop into thin slices. Sauté gently in the olive oil and add the coriander. When the vegetables are slightly translucent, remove from the heat.

Roll out the pastry to fit a medium-sized quiche dish, and spread the vegetables evenly over the pastry. Chop the nuts and scatter over the vegetables. Whisk the eggs and milk, add the grated cheese, salt and pepper, and pour over the vegetables. Place in a preheated oven, Gas Mark 4, 180°C, 350°F, and bake for 45 minutes until fully set and golden brown. Serve with jacket potatoes and a green salad.

CHESTNUT CASSEROLE

Chestnuts are extremely versatile and can be used in both savoury and sweet dishes. I often make chestnut soufflé, using the same recipe as the parsnip and onion soufflé (page 112). This casserole can be prepared well in advance and it also freezes well. Tins of whole chestnuts are widely available in supermarkets, and dried chestnuts are available in health food shops.

283 g (10 oz) tin of whole chestnuts or dried chestnuts	2 cloves garlic
	olive oil
150 g (6 oz) parsnips	2 tablespoons parsley, chopped
150 g (6 oz) swedes or turnips	1 tablespoon oregano, chopped
100 g (4 oz) potatoes	3 tablespoons shoyu sauce
100 g (4 oz) mushrooms	1 wine glass white wine
2 onions	3 tablespoons white wine vinegar
3 carrots	juice of 1 lemon
3 courgettes	2 tablespoons brown sugar
1 green pepper	salt and freshly ground pepper

Soak the dried chestnuts overnight, drain and wash, then boil for 10 minutes and simmer for 1 hour. If you are using tinned chestnuts, soak in freshly boiled water for 5 minutes.

Peel and chop the parsnips, swedes and potatoes. Boil and then simmer until slightly soft. Drain thoroughly. Wipe the mushrooms and chop into large pieces. Chop the onions, carrots, courgettes and green pepper and sauté gently with the crushed garlic in the olive oil for 5 minutes. If they look dry, add some extra olive oil. Add the parsley, oregano and the well-drained chestnuts, parsnips, swedes and potatoes and cook for 2 minutes. Mix all the liquid ingredients together with the brown sugar, pour over the vegetables, and cook for 3 minutes. Remove from the heat.

Transfer to a greased ovenproof dish. Stir in 250 ml (½ pint) of water, and season. Cover the dish and cook in a preheated oven, Gas Mark 4, 180°C, 350°F, for 20 minutes. If the mixture looks too dry, add a further 125 ml (¼ pint) of water. Remove the cover and cook for an additional 15 minutes.

CHICK PEA PASTA

300 g (12 oz) chick peas
2 cloves garlic
2 onions
1 green pepper
150 g (6 oz) mushrooms
4 large courgettes
6 carrots
100 g (4 oz) green beans
olive oil
6 tablespoons parsley, chopped

6 tablespoons coriander, chopped
½ teaspoon marjoram, chopped
½ teaspoon thyme, chopped
½ teaspoon oregano, chopped
2 tablespoons lemon juice
salt and freshly ground pepper
500 g (1 lb) pasta (of your choice)
100 g (4 oz) freshly grated
　　Parmesan cheese

Soak the chick peas overnight, rinse, drain, then boil for 10 minutes and simmer for 1 hour.

Prepare all the vegetables and chop into chunky pieces. Crush the garlic. Sauté the garlic and onions in the olive oil for 2 minutes. Add the mushrooms and courgettes, then the carrots, green pepper, beans, parsley, coriander and the other herbs. Cook gently for 5 minutes. Add the drained chick peas. Simmer for 20 minutes and then add the lemon juice, salt and pepper. Add olive oil if the mixture appears dry.

Boil a large saucepan of water. Cook the pasta for 15 minutes, and drain thoroughly. Pour the vegetable sauce over the pasta and sprinkle with a little cheese. Pass the rest of the cheese round in a small bowl. A well-dressed green salad goes well with this.

COUSCOUS AND VEGETABLES

Couscous is a type of fine semolina which is very popular in North African countries. It is rather complicated and fiddly to cook but, thanks to the North African influence in France, it is now possible to buy precooked couscous which just needs steaming. (It is sold in many supermarkets, usually alongside the rice and pulses, and has 'couscous medium precooked' on the packet.) The vegetables can be varied depending on availability but I always include onions, carrots and courgettes for a good, strong flavour. I often make large quantities of the vegetables and freeze half.

250 g (8 oz) onions	olive oil
250 g (8 oz) courgettes	1 teaspoon each of cumin,
250 g (8 oz) carrots	paprika, turmeric or saffron
1 large aubergine	salt and freshly ground pepper
3 large potatoes	250 g (8 oz) chick peas (cooked)
250 g (8 oz) tomatoes	100 g (4 oz) dates
4 tablespoons parsley	100 g (4 oz) raisins
4 tablespoons coriander	500 g (1 lb) couscous (precooked)
2 cloves garlic	

Prepare and chop all the vegetables into big chunky pieces. Chop the parsley and coriander and crush the garlic. Gently heat the olive oil and cook the vegetables and herbs very slowly until they are soft. Add 125 ml (¼ pint) of water, the cumin, paprika, turmeric or saffron, salt and pepper. Add the chick peas, dates and raisins. Simmer for 20 minutes.

In the meantime, prepare the couscous. Put it in a bowl, add salt and pepper, and about 500 ml (1 pint) boiling water. Leave to settle for at least 10 minutes, and then fluff the grains with a fork. (The soaking and fluffing is to stop the grains sticking together.) To steam the couscous, transfer it to a saucepan that fits snugly into a larger one beneath, in which there is boiling water. The base of the top pan should sit above the level of the water. Add 2 tablespoons of olive oil to the couscous and steam (the length of time required will depend on the size of your pan, among other things, but I find that by the time the water in the bottom pan has come back to a furious boil the couscous is done).

Serve the couscous on a large dish with the vegetables spooned on top. Couscous is traditionally eaten with harissa, a very strong, hot pepper sauce, available in grocers (it is often stocked by Asian grocers). Be very cautious with this as it can burn your mouth if you are not used to it.

FENNEL DELIGHT

Fennel is another much-neglected vegetable in Britain. I use it raw in salads or cook it as an accompanying vegetable. This is a favourite supper dish which is quick to prepare.

Pastry	*Filling*
200 g (8 oz) wholemeal flour	4 fennel
50 g (2 oz) butter or margarine (must be cold)	150 g (6 oz) Feta cheese
	salt and freshly ground pepper
cold water	150 g (6 oz) butter or margarine
½ teaspoon salt	

Add the salt to the flour and rub the butter into the flour until it forms crumbs. Slowly pour in a little cold water and stir until it forms a dough. Knead with your hand into a ball and wrap in foil. Place immediately in the fridge.

Meanwhile, prepare the filling. Trim the fennel of any feathery tops and remove any bruised bits. Chop. Bring a saucepan of water to the boil and simmer the fennel for about 15 minutes or until they are *al dente* (slightly soft but with a bite). Drain. Roll out the pastry and line a buttered ovenproof dish. Spread the fennel evenly over the base. Crumble the Feta cheese and scatter over the fennel. Add salt and lots of black pepper and dot with butter. Cook in a preheated oven at Gas Mark 4, 180°C, 350°F, until lightly browned (about 25 minutes).

Note:
This dish is just as good cooked without the pastry base, if you prefer.

HAZELNUT AND VEGETABLE PILAF

The vegetables can be varied according to taste and availability. Apart from those listed below, try broccoli (Calabrese), cauliflower, carrots, runner beans, mangetout, potatoes, red and yellow peppers or watercress in different combinations. I don't recommend Brussels sprouts or cabbage as their flavour tends to dominate. In place of the hazelnuts, walnuts, almonds, pine nuts, cashew or brazil nuts are all equally successful.

150 g (6 oz) mushrooms	300 g (12 oz) hazelnuts
150 g (6 oz) courgettes	olive oil
150 g (6 oz) tomatoes	1 tablespoon tarragon, chopped
2 leeks	500 g (1 lb) long grain brown rice
2 onions	salt and freshly ground pepper
1 green pepper	3 tablespoons coriander or
3 cloves garlic	parsley, chopped
	2 teaspoons saffron or turmeric

Prepare and chop the vegetables and crush the garlic. Crush the hazelnuts gently, taking care not to make the pieces too small. Heat a generous quantity of olive oil and cook all the vegetables, except the tomatoes, and the tarragon gently for a few minutes until they look glazed. Stir in the rice, tomatoes, nuts, salt, pepper and coriander and cook for an extra minute, adding more olive oil if it looks dry. Add 1 litre (2 pints) of water, boil for 10 minutes and add the saffron or turmeric (for its lovely colour). Cover tightly and simmer for 45 minutes.

If, after 45 minutes, the surface is not pitted with small holes, replace the lid and continue to cook for another 15 minutes, without touching the rice. Never stir rice in mid-cooking or it will become starchy. Once it is cooked, switch off the heat, and leave in the lidded pan for another 30 minutes or more. This dries out the dish and improves the flavour. To reheat, transfer to an ovenproof dish and place in a medium-hot oven, Gas Mark 4, 180°C, 350°F, for 15 minutes.

LEEKS CROUSTADE

Leeks taste especially good in this croustade, although you can follow the recipe with other vegetables. It is similar to a quiche but much lighter.

3 slices granary bread
6 large leeks
olive oil
1 clove garlic, crushed
2 tablespoons parsley, chopped
150 g (6 oz) cheese (choose your favourite from Edam, Feta, Gouda or Parmesan)

50 g (2 oz) margarine
2 eggs
3 tablespoons single cream or milk
salt and freshly ground pepper

First lightly toast the bread and make breadcrumbs, in a food processor, or by putting the toast into a bag and crushing with a rolling pin.

Wash the leeks thoroughly. Cut into chunky pieces and leave in just-boiled water for 15 minutes, rinse and leave to dry. Heat the olive oil and sauté the leeks and the crushed garlic gently until lightly browned. Add the parsley and cook for a few more minutes. Butter a pie dish. Mix the grated cheese with the breadcrumbs. Melt the margarine and add the cheese breadcrumbs, mix well, then spread over the base of the pie dish. Press it down with a fork so that it completely covers the base. Place the leek mixture on top. Beat the eggs with the milk or cream, season, and pour over the leeks. Bake in a preheated oven for 40 minutes at Gas Mark 4, 180°C, 350°F, for 35 minutes until golden brown.

LENTIL HOTPOT

A marvellous cheering hotpot for cold days, as colourful as it is tasty!

2 cloves garlic	200 g (8 oz) red lentils
2 onions	olive oil
3 potatoes	1 teaspoon thyme, chopped
4 courgettes	2 tablespoons yeast extract
3 carrots	salt and freshly ground pepper
5 tomatoes	

Prepare and chop all the vegetables. Wash the lentils. Gently heat the olive oil and add the garlic, onions, potatoes, courgettes and carrots. When they are slightly brown, add the lentils, thyme and tomatoes, yeast extract, salt, pepper and 4 tablespoons of water. Cook for 5 more minutes. Transfer to an ovenproof dish, add 125 ml (¼ pint) of water and place in a preheated oven, Gas Mark 4, 180°C, 350°F, for 1 hour. (It may also be simmered on top of the cooker for 1 hour, but I think cooking in the oven produces a better flavour.)

LENTILS WITH VEGETABLES

This simple Middle Eastern dish was introduced to me in Israel. The smell of coriander, garlic and onion produces the most wonderful aroma that always reminds me of my Jerusalem kitchen. Lentils are a valuable, cheap source of protein and carbohydrates, containing essential vitamins, iron and calcium, and have long been known as a cure for anaemia. They are also delicious and very easy to cook. Red lentils are not suitable for this dish (they go rather mushy) but green or brown ones are perfect. Experiment with different combinations of vegetables. In addition to those listed, I often add mangetout, peppers and runner beans.

I never bother to measure rice; I use a standard teacup which takes about 100 g (4 oz) rice, and then cook the rice in double the amount of water, i.e. two teacups.

500 g (1 lb) green or brown lentils	6 courgettes
olive oil	4 carrots
3 cloves garlic, crushed	200 g (8 oz) mushrooms
300 g (12 oz) long grain rice, washed	200 g (8 oz) green beans
2 tablespoons pine nuts	4 tablespoons coriander
4 large onions	4 tablespoons parsley
	salt and freshly ground pepper

Soak the lentils overnight, or for a minimum of 4 hours, drain and rinse carefully. Place in a large saucepan with cold water and bring to the boil. Simmer for 1½ hours.

In a separate saucepan, heat the olive oil and cook one clove of crushed garlic. Add the rice and cook for a minute, then the pine nuts. When they are slightly cooked, add water. (Use the same cup as you measured the rice in and use exactly double the amount of water.) Bring to the boil for 5 minutes, cover with a tight-fitting lid and simmer for 30 minutes until all the water is absorbed and the surface is pitted.

Meanwhile, prepare and chop all the vegetables and herbs, and cook very gently in the olive oil with the rest of the crushed garlic until they are soft (about 10 minutes) and nearly caramelised. Drain the lentils and mix with the vegetables. Serve over the hot rice.

In the Middle East, it is common to cook 2 or 3 extra onions, sliced into rings, in olive oil until they are very brown and sticky and serve these on top.

MUSHROOM AND CURD CHEESE MARJORAM PIE

Use button mushrooms if possible in this delicately flavoured flan.

Pastry	*Filling*
200 g (8 oz) flour	300 g (12 oz) mushrooms
100 g (4 oz) butter or margarine	2 onions
cold water (preferably ice cold)	1 clove garlic
salt	1 tablespoon marjoram, chopped
	olive oil
	200 g (8 oz) curd cheese
	3 eggs
	salt and freshly ground pepper
	nutmeg

To make the pastry, mix the flour and salt in a basin. Chop the cold margarine or butter into little pieces, and rub into the flour to form crumbs. Add a little water slowly until the mixture forms a dough. Roll into a ball, wrap in clingfilm or silver foil and leave in the fridge for a minimum of 30 minutes (chilled dough is much easier to handle).

Wipe and slice the mushrooms, including the stalks. Peel and chop the onions and garlic. Over a very low heat, sauté the mushrooms, onions, garlic and marjoram in the olive oil until soft. Beat the cheese and eggs together until smooth. Season. Roll out the pastry into a flan dish and spread the vegetable mixture over the base. Add the cheese and egg mixture, sprinkle nutmeg on top and bake at Gas Mark 4, 180°C, 350°F, for 45 minutes.

Note:
Cream cheese will give a richer taste and Feta cheese is also good in this pie. Experiment with other varieties too.

MUSHROOMS IN FILO PASTRY

This is a dish to make for special occasions. It is time-consuming but is really worth the effort. Once cooked, it will freeze excellently, and you can make and freeze large quantities of it for parties.

Filo pastry (sometimes called strudel or phillo pastry) can be bought frozen in many supermarkets, and it can be bought fresh from some Greek and Cypriot groceries and bakers. If you haven't cooked with it before, make a small quantity of this dish the first time. Once you get the hang of it, however, you will be able to make lots of wonderful savoury and sweet dishes.

There are two important rules to remember when cooking with filo:

1. It must never be allowed to dry out. Once defrosted, wrap it in a damp teacloth until it is all used up. I start to use it when it is not completely defrosted to stop it becoming dry. This sounds odd, but you will see that it is very pliable then.
2. Each layer of filo must be lavishly brushed with butter. This is essential for the success of the dish, otherwise it will dry out during baking. As a lot of butter is used in the cooking of filo pastry (and margarine really doesn't taste the same), I always cook the vegetables in olive oil to lower the cholesterol level of the meal.

The sauce can be omitted, if you like (I only make it for special occasions), as the mushroom filo is delicious on its own too, either hot or chilled.

---

500 g (1 lb) filo pastry
1 kilo (2 lb) mushrooms
2 onions
3 cloves garlic
olive oil
2 tablespoons thyme, chopped
6 eggs
500 g (1 lb) Feta cheese (or
   Ricotta if you don't like Feta)
pepper
100 g (4 oz) butter

Sauce
4 onions
50 g (2 oz) butter
1 tablespoon cornflour
250 ml (½ pint) single cream or
   Greek yoghourt
2 tablespoons sherry or vermouth

You will also need:
a square or rectangular oven dish, about 25 cm × 31 cm × 7 cm
(10 in × 12 in × 3 in)
a pastry brush

Take the filo pastry out of the freezer 1½ hours before you start to cook. Wipe the mushrooms and remove the stalks. Peel and chop the onion and crush the garlic. Heat the olive oil, and add the mushrooms, garlic and onions and cook very slowly until soft. Add the thyme.

While they are cooking, mix together the eggs, Feta cheese and a generous sprinkling of pepper. Butter the oven dish. Melt the butter in a separate saucepan. Open up the filo pastry until it is flat. Lay one sheet of the filo pastry across the base of the dish. Leave the extra length extending over the edge. Brush generously with the melted butter, and work along the length of the dish, overlapping each sheet of filo and brushing each generously with butter.

When you have completed one side, turn the dish and work along the next in the same manner. When you have finished all the pastry there should be ends extending over each side. Arrange the mushroom mixture evenly over the pastry and pour over the eggs and Feta.

Carefully fold over the loose pieces of pastry to enclose the filling, again brushing each sheet with melted butter. When you have finished, brush the top with butter and with a very sharp knife cut through the top layer of pastry in three or four places. This allows the filling to come through when baking and gives an attractive finish. Place in a preheated oven, Gas Mark 5, 190°C, 370°F, for about 50 minutes until golden brown. Leave to settle for a few minutes.

To make the sauce, peel and chop the onions. Melt the butter and very slowly sauté the onion until it becomes translucent. Add 4 tablespoons of cold water to the cornflour to make a paste. Stir this into the onions until the mixture thickens. Cook for an extra minute. Pour in the cream or yoghourt and stir slowly, until thickened. Add the vermouth or sherry and cook for an extra minute.

Cut the mushroom filo into thick square pieces and serve with the hot sauce.

MUSHROOM PILAF

An easy way to measure rice and the amount of water you need to cook it in is to use a teacup: one teacup will hold approximately 100 g (4 oz) rice, and you need double the volume – two teacups – of water to cook it in.

3 onions	olive oil
500 g (1 lb) mushrooms	200 g (8 oz) long grain brown rice
3 tomatoes	2 tablespoons yeast extract
3 tablespoons parsley	salt and freshly ground pepper
3 tablespoons coriander	2 wine glasses white wine
2 cloves garlic	

Prepare and chop the vegetables and herbs, and crush the garlic. In a large saucepan, heat the olive oil and gently sauté the mushrooms, onions and garlic. When they are lightly browned, add the coriander and most of the parsley, reserving a little for decoration. Cook for another minute.

Add the tomatoes and the washed rice to the mixture and cook for 1 minute. Add water (as described in the note above), the yeast extract, salt and pepper and bring to the boil for 5 minutes. Reduce to a very low heat and add the wine. Cover the saucepan with a tight-fitting lid and simmer for 30 minutes. Do not lift the lid or touch the rice (if you stir it, it will become starchy and sticky). After 30 minutes, the rice should be dry and the surface pitted. If not, simmer for a further 15 minutes.

Sprinkle the reserved parsley over. I like to serve this with a well-dressed lettuce, endive, radicchio and onion salad.

MUSHROOM STROGANOFF

This is one of my favourite dishes to serve to guests. It does not take long to make and is really delicious. It can be made quite easily in large quantities and so is useful for parties and large family gatherings. If you do not like eating cream you may use yoghourt – try to buy the Greek-style yoghourt.

When I cook rice I use two parts water to one part rice, and I measure these quantities in a teacup, which holds roughly 100 g (4 oz) rice. It is a failproof method of having just the right amount of water.

300 g (12 oz) long-grain brown rice
3 large onions
4 cloves garlic
500 g (1 lb) mushrooms, preferably button
olive oil

2 teaspoons thyme, chopped
4 tablespoons parsley, chopped
salt and freshly ground pepper
1 wine glass white wine
250 ml (½ pint) cream or Greek yoghourt

Wash the rice in cold water (and measure the amount of water you will need for cooking it; see above). Heat a tablespoon of olive oil in a saucepan and cook one of the cloves of garlic, crushed. Add the rice and cook for a further minute. Add the cooking water to the pan, bring to the boil and boil for 10 minutes. Add salt and pepper and cover with a tight-fitting lid. Turn down the heat and simmer for 30 minutes. When done, the surface of the rice should be pitted with little holes. Leave the pan covered so that the rice can continue to dry out until you need it.

Meanwhile, peel and slice the onions, and the remaining garlic. Wipe and slice the mushrooms. Gently heat the olive oil and slowly soften the vegetables, garlic and herbs. When the vegetables are just cooked, add a little salt and a generous sprinkling of pepper. Add the wine and cook for a couple of minutes. Remove from the heat and stir in the cream or yoghourt. Return to the heat for just long enough to warm the cream or yoghourt. Serve immediately with the hot rice.

OKRA AND TOMATO PILAF

This is a variation of a dish eaten all over the Middle East. Okra (bamia) is also known as lady's fingers – you will see why when you buy them. They have become more commonly available in Britain as they are used in many Greek and Asian dishes. I find them now very easy to obtain in my local supermarket although they are often unlabelled and stuck away in a corner, along with lots of other interesting-looking fruits and vegetables. I have discovered şome wonderful recipes and new delights by talking to Asian ladies in this section, and I cannot understand why these fruits and vegetables are not better marketed in this country.

---

500 g (1 lb) long grain brown rice
olive oil
4 cloves garlic, crushed
salt and freshly ground pepper
2 teaspoons turmeric or saffron
1 kilo (2 lb) okra
500 g (1 lb) small onions

500 g (1 lb) tomatoes
3 tablespoons crushed coriander
  seeds (or ground coriander can
  be used if seeds are not
  available)
juice of 2 lemons

Wash the okra, remove the stalks, and chop. Peel and slice the onions into rings and the tomatoes into thick slices. Heat the olive oil. Add the onions and cook on a low heat until lightly browned. Add the okra and three cloves of crushed garlic and continue to cook until the vegetables are slightly soft. Add the tomatoes and coriander seeds for another 2 minutes. Season. Add just enough water to cover the vegetables and simmer for 45 minutes.

Meanwhile, wash the rice thoroughly and drain. Measure twice its volume in water. Heat some olive oil in a saucepan and gently cook the rest of the garlic. When slightly soft add the rice and water, bring to the boil and boil for 10 minutes. Add salt, pepper and the saffron or turmeric. Cover with a tight-fitting lid and simmer for 30 minutes.

Add half the lemon juice to the vegetable mixture and continue to cook for another 10 minutes. Sprinkle the remaining lemon juice over the vegetables and serve with the hot rice.

PARSNIP AND ONION SOUFFLÉ

I love parsnips and am always surprised that they are not used more in cooking in this country. This soufflé is really not difficult to make: the secrets of successful soufflé-making are a preheated oven and a closed oven door while cooking!

300 g (12 oz) potatoes	2 tablespoons coriander, chopped
300 g (12 oz) parsnips	(use fresh parsley if you can't
2 onions	find coriander)
50 g (2 oz) butter or margarine	½ teaspoon mustard
50 g (2 oz) flour	50 g (2 oz) freshly grated
150 ml (¼ pint) single cream or	Parmesan cheese
yoghourt	salt and freshly ground pepper
5 eggs, separated (use 4 yolks,	
5 egg whites)	

Preheat the oven to Gas Mark 4, 180°C, 350°F, and make sure that the shelves are arranged so that there is space for the soufflé dish in the middle of the oven; if you do this later, when putting the soufflé into the oven, you will lose valuable heat. Place an empty baking tray in the oven (this acts as a hot base for the soufflé and really does seem to improve it). Grease a large soufflé dish (1½ litres/ 3 pints). Peel the potatoes and parsnips and boil until soft. Peel and finely chop the onions and purée or mash with the vegetables. Melt the butter or margarine and stir in the flour until it makes a thick paste. Add the cream very slowly, mixing well to make a smooth sauce. Remove from the heat.*

Stir in the egg yolks thoroughly then add the coriander, mustard, puréed vegetables, grated cheese, salt and pepper. Beat the egg whites stiffly and slowly fold into the mixture, using a metal spoon. Turn into the soufflé dish and place the dish on the heated baking tray. Bake for 40 minutes.

If the soufflé seems very wobbly when you (carefully) open the oven, close the door and leave for a further 15 minutes (it might deflate but will taste all right). Eat immediately.

*If you wish to prepare the soufflé in advance, you may do so up to this point. If you are preparing it more than a couple of hours in advance, keep the mixture in the fridge in a covered bowl. Reheat it gently before you continue with the recipe.

PASTA AND PEPPER SAUCE

A quick dish to prepare in a hurry or for unexpected guests, which will transport you to the Mediterranean, even if it is pouring outside! To make it particularly attractive, use different-coloured peppers and the three-coloured pasta (orange, yellow and green) that is meant to resemble the Italian flag; or you can use home-made pasta available from Italian grocers, in which case it will need cooking for only a few minutes, not ten as for dried pasta.

3 large onions	½ teaspoon each basil, oregano
2 cloves garlic	and marjoram, chopped
6 peppers (try different colours)	500 g (1 lb) pasta
olive oil	salt and freshly ground pepper

Boil the water for the pasta. Peel and slice the onions and garlic. Slice the peppers. Gently heat the olive oil and add the chopped vegetables and garlic. After 2 minutes add the herbs. Start to cook the pasta, adding a little oil to prevent it sticking. Continue to cook the vegetables very slowly (adding olive oil if dry) until they are soft, which takes about 10 minutes. Season. Drain the pasta, pour the sauce over and serve with a green salad, garlic bread and a bottle of dry white wine.

PUMPKIN PIE

Pumpkin has a fine delicate flavour, shown to advantage in this delectable pie.

Filling	Pastry
750 g (1½ lb) pumpkin	75 g (3 oz) butter or margarine
1 onion	200 g (8 oz) wholemeal flour
1 tablespoon oregano, chopped	salt and freshly ground pepper
salt and freshly ground pepper	cold water
3 eggs, beaten	
5 tablespoons single cream or yoghourt	

First of all, cut the pumpkin in half and remove the seeds. Place in a medium-hot oven, Gas Mark 4, 180°C, 350°F, for 1 hour to soften the flesh. Allow to cool a little and scoop the flesh into a bowl.

Start to make the pastry while the pumpkin is cooking. Cut the butter into thick, small pieces, and rub into the flour until it forms crumbs. Add cold water slowly until it forms a pastry ball. Wrap in foil and leave in the fridge for a minimum of 30 minutes.

Peel and chop the onion finely and add it to the pumpkin flesh. Add the oregano, salt, pepper and the beaten eggs. Slowly add the cream and mix well. Roll out two-thirds of the pastry and line an ovenproof dish. Pile the pumpkin mixture over the pastry. Roll the remaining dough out very thinly and place over the mixture. Press the corners together with water. Cut a cross-type vent in the middle of the pie. If you like glazed pies, brush with beaten yolk or milk. Place in a preheated oven, Gas Mark 4, 180°C, 350°F, for 50 minutes until golden brown.

Note:
If you prefer, you can omit the pie lid and cook in a flan dish for a quiche-type pie.

PUMPKIN AND BURGHUL PIE

I have learned of many wonderful new dishes and ways of using vegetables from friends offering me their favourite recipes for this book. This one came from my hairdresser Steve and my oldest schoolfriend, Georgina. It is a Greek Cypriot dish, known as *Kolokodes* in Greek, and is traditionally made in individual pasties. I found this too time-consuming so I make it as a pie. Use white flour for the pastry as it becomes very heavy if made with wholemeal.

Pastry	*Filling*
200 g (8 oz) white flour	200 g (8 oz) sultanas
75 g (3 oz) butter or margarine	750 g (1½ lb) pumpkin
1 egg yolk, beaten, to glaze (optional)	100 g (4 oz) burghul (sometimes called cracked wheat or bulgar)
cold water	1 tablespoon cinnamon

Cut the pumpkin in two, remove seeds and cut flesh into chunks. Salt thoroughly and leave for several hours to soften the flesh. Make the pastry. Rub the butter into the flour until it forms crumbs. Add a few drops of water at a time until it becomes a dough. Knead and then wrap in foil. Place in fridge to rest until required.

Place the sultanas in freshly boiled water for 10 minutes. Wash the pumpkin chunks to remove the salt and drain. Mash the flesh with the rinsed burghul. Leave for a few minutes. Add the cinnamon and the sultanas to the mixture. Roll out the pastry on a floured board. Line the base of a pie dish with half the pastry, pile the pumpkin mixture over and cover with the remaining pastry.

If you wish, you can brush the top with the beaten yolk of an egg to give an attractive glaze. Cook in a preheated oven, Gas Mark 4, 180°C, 350°F, for 45 minutes.

SPAGHETTI ALLA PIRATA

A vegetarian version of a dish from the south-west coast of Italy, famous for its pirates. It is normally made with anchovies and olives.

3 cloves garlic	olive oil
200 g (8 oz) mushrooms	2 tablespoons parsley, chopped
1 red pepper	1 tablespoon basil, chopped
300 g (12 oz) black olives	salt and freshly ground pepper
300 g (12 oz) spaghetti	

Peel and chop the garlic finely. Wipe and slice the mushrooms and chop the red pepper. Quarter the black olives and remove the pits. Cook the spaghetti in a pan of boiling water, adding a little oil to prevent it sticking.

While the spaghetti cooks, heat the olive oil and add the garlic, mushrooms, olives and red pepper. Cook slowly for 3 minutes. Add the parsley, basil, salt and pepper. Cook for another 3 minutes. If the sauce becomes dry, add more olive oil. Serve very hot over the drained spaghetti.

SPANAKOPITTA
(Spinach and Feta in Filo Pastry)

Although this takes some time to prepare, it is a wonderful party dish and is well worth the effort. If you have not used filo pastry before, do have a practice run. It can be bought frozen in supermarkets, or if you live in an area with a Greek or Cypriot population you might be able to buy it fresh (it is sometimes called phillo or strudel pastry).

Spanakopitta freezes very well and can be made in large quantities for parties. I make it and freeze it in very large Portuguese earthenware dishes. If you do freeze it, remember that it takes a long time to defrost. I remove it from the freezer the morning of an evening meal and leave it in the fridge. Three hours before eating, I check to see if it has defrosted. If not, I leave it out of the fridge. To reheat once defrosted, place the dish in a preheated oven, Gas Mark 4, 180°C, 350°F, for 45 minutes.

---

500 g (1 lb) filo pastry
1 kilo (2 lbs) spinach (you may use frozen but never tinned)
2 onions
1 clove garlic
olive oil

1 tablespoon thyme, chopped
7 eggs
500 g (1 lb) Feta cheese, crumbled
freshly ground pepper
150 g (6 oz) butter

You will also need:
a square or rectangular oven dish, about 25 cm × 31 cm × 7 cm (10 in × 12 in × 3 in)
a pastry brush

Defrost the filo pastry for 1½–2 hours. Don't be tempted to take it out several hours before; if it becomes dry it will become too brittle to use. If something prevents you using it within two hours, wrap it in a wet teacloth and leave it in the fridge.

Wash the spinach thoroughly, place in a saucepan, and simmer gently for 15 minutes. (The water clinging to the leaves produces sufficient moisture.) Drain.

Peel and chop the onions and garlic. Sauté in olive oil with the thyme until lightly browned. Mix well with the eggs, crumbled Feta cheese, spinach and pepper. (I do this in seconds in a food processor.) You do not need additional salt as there is plenty in the Feta cheese.

Take a large square or rectangular ovenproof dish, just a bit smaller than the opened filo pastry. Gently melt the butter, and lay the filo pastry out flat. Brush the baking dish with a thin layer of melted butter. Lay one sheet of filo pastry across the dish, with the extra extending over both sides. Brush with butter. Work your way along one side of the dish, overlapping the sheets of filo and brushing each with butter. Turn the dish and repeat in the other direction. You should have lengths of pastry extending all round the dish.

Pour in the filling. Carefully fold the pastry over the filling, again brushing each sheet with butter. When all the pastry ends are folded over, brush the top thoroughly with butter. Then cut through the top layers in several straight lines with a sharp knife. This allows the filling to come through. Bake at Gas Mark 5, 190°C, 375°F, for about 50 minutes, until golden brown. Serve cut into large squares.

STUFFED ARTICHOKES

When we lived in Jerusalem, my husband John and I often used to eat at an unusual, cosy little restaurant run by a marvellously eccentric Bulgarian cook. No menu was displayed and he served whatever he had cooked that day, his *pièce de résistance* being stuffed vegetables, of which several types were cooked at every meal: courgettes, carrots, peppers, aubergines, onions and artichokes. I give the recipe for stuffing aubergines, peppers or courgettes opposite, but this version is delightfully different.

4 artichokes	olive oil
2 onions	2 tablespoons coriander, chopped
2 cloves garlic	2 tablespoons shoyu sauce
2 slices granary bread	juice of 1 lemon
200 g (8 oz) hazelnuts or walnuts	salt and freshly ground pepper

Remove the stems from the artichokes. Boil the artichokes for 10 minutes then simmer for 50 minutes.

Peel and chop the onions and crush the garlic. Toast the bread and make breadcrumbs (in a food processor, or place in a bag and crush with a rolling pin). Chop the nuts. Heat some olive oil in a saucepan. Cook the onion and garlic for 5 minutes and then add the coriander, nuts and breadcrumbs for another 3 minutes. Stir in the shoyu sauce and 6 tablespoons of water. Cook for another 3 minutes. If the mixture becomes dry at any time, add more olive oil. Remove the pan from the heat and stir in the lemon juice, a little salt and lots of pepper.

As soon as the artichokes have cooked, place them in a sieve and allow them to drain well. Carefully prise apart the top leaves of each artichoke, removing any centre leaves if necessary to expose the choke. Remove the hairy choke with a teaspoon. Divide the stuffing between the artichokes and press down firmly into the hollow left by the removal of the choke.

Place the artichokes in an ovenproof dish. Fit them together tightly so that they remain upright. Cover with silver foil and cook in a preheated oven, Gas Mark 4, 180°C, 350°F, for 30 minutes.

STUFFED AUBERGINES (COURGETTES OR PEPPERS)

This recipe can be used for stuffing aubergines, courgettes or peppers. Courgettes and peppers should be sprinkled with salt and left for one hour to soften the skins. If you are stuffing courgettes, you will need three medium-sized courgettes per person. Use a grapefruit knife to remove the inner flesh; cut this into small chunks and salt for half an hour to remove the bitter juice. One large pepper is sufficient per person; simply cut off the top and remove the seeds. Onions can also be stuffed following this recipe. All freeze well, so it is worth making double the specified quantity.

2 large aubergines	*Sauce*
2 large onions	2 large onions
3 cloves garlic	1 clove garlic
5 tablespoons parsley, chopped	olive oil
olive oil	4 tablespoons parsley, chopped
6 tomatoes	6 tomatoes (or 1 350 g (14 oz)
100 g (4 oz) pine nuts	can)
300 g (12 oz) long grain brown	2 tablespoons tomato purée
rice, washed	salt and freshly ground pepper
1 tablespoon ground cumin	
salt and freshly ground pepper	

Cut the aubergines in half lengthways, and scoop out the flesh, making sure the shells remain intact. Put the shells aside and sprinkle a lot of salt inside them. Put the flesh in a colander and salt generously. Leave with a heavy weight on top for a minimum of 2 hours (I use a saucepan filled with water) to remove the bitter juices. The flesh is not required in this recipe, but retain and use for the aubergine and tahini spread on page 122.

Peel and slice the onions and garlic and sauté with the parsley in the olive oil until lightly browned. Chop the tomatoes and add to the pan, together with the pine nuts and the washed rice, cumin, salt and pepper. (If you like cumin, you might like to add an extra

121

tablespoon.) Cook on a very low heat for 2–3 minutes. Do not stir too much as this makes the rice starchy. Add ½ litre (1 pint) of water. Bring slowly to the boil, reduce the heat, cover and allow to simmer for 30 minutes. When all the water is absorbed, turn off the heat and leave for another 30 minutes with the lid on to allow the rice to dry out (this really seems to work wonders, producing a better-flavoured, drier rice).

Wash and dry the aubergine (or courgette/pepper) shells and stuff with the rice mixture. Only stuff three-quarters full as the mixture expands. Pack the aubergines closely into a greased deep oven-proof dish and pour water into it to reach three-quarters up the side of the aubergines. Cover the dish with silver foil and bake in the middle of a preheated oven, Gas Mark 5, 190°C, 375°F, for 1¾ hours. Remove the foil after 1 hour. At the end of the cooking time, the aubergines should be very well cooked. If they are not, leave for a further 15 minutes.

Meanwhile, make the tomato sauce. Peel and chop the onions and garlic into small pieces, and gently sauté in olive oil until they are lightly browned. Add the parsley and cook for an extra minute, then add the tomatoes, tomato purée, salt and pepper. Leave to simmer for 30 minutes. Serve very hot, poured over the aubergines, with a well-dressed lettuce and onion or red and green pepper salad, and perhaps some extra rice.

You will still have the aubergine flesh. With this you can make the delicious spread below.

AUBERGINE AND TAHINI SPREAD

This spread is useful for using up the aubergine flesh from stuffed aubergines (see above). However, it's so good it's worth buying aubergines specially for this recipe. It will keep in the fridge in an airtight container for up to a week.

flesh of 2 large aubergines	juice of 1 lemon
olive oil	2 cloves garlic
4 tablespoons tahini paste	salt and freshly ground pepper

If you have not already made the stuffed aubergine dish (above), then do the following to obtain the flesh. Put 2 aubergines in a medium hot oven, Gas Mark 4, 180°C, 350°F, for 45 minutes, then run the aubergines under the cold tap to remove the skin. Put the flesh in a colander, sprinkle with salt, and cover with a heavy weight. Leave for 2 hours to remove the bitter juices. Rinse well. (In Middle Eastern countries the aubergine is put on a naked flame or grilled and allowed to burn. Then the skins are washed off. I have prepared aubergines in this way on the gas at home and the taste is wonderful, but it is messy and not really worth the clearing up afterwards.)

If you have made the stuffed aubergine, then sauté the aubergine flesh for 2 or 3 minutes in olive oil until lightly browned all over. Cooked aubergine changes colour very rapidly and so you will easily be able to see when it is cooked.

Put all the ingredients into a blender or processor and mix until smooth, or use a potato masher. Taste, and add extra lemon juice if required. If the mixture is very thick, add water slowly. Keep in the fridge for at least an hour before serving with hot pitta bread.

STUFFED VINE LEAVES

This dish is rather fiddly to make but the effort is worth it. Vine leaves are occasionally available fresh in Greek or Turkish grocers, but they are more commonly bought preserved in brine, in sealed packets, from grocers and supermarkets. I usually make large quantities and freeze half, which I then serve as a starter, rather than a main course. The quantity in this recipe makes about 60 small stuffed vine leaves.

2 packets vine leaves (or fresh if available)
300 g (12 oz) wholegrain rice
2 onions
2 cloves garlic
3 tomatoes
3 tablespoons parsley
3 tablespoons mint
100 g (4 oz) pine nuts

1 teaspoon allspice
1 teaspoon cinnamon
1 teaspoon saffron or ½ teaspoon turmeric
salt and freshly ground pepper
juice of 2 lemons
2 tablespoons brown sugar
8 tablespoons olive oil

If you are using vine leaves preserved in brine, it is essential that you remove the brine taste. To do this, rinse the leaves thoroughly in a sieve. Then take a large bowl, fill with boiling water, immerse the leaves for 30 minutes and then throw the water away. Add fresh boiled water to the leaves for an extra 15 minutes. Then sieve all the water away and leave in cold water until you start to cook. If you are using fresh leaves, soak them in boiling water for 5 minutes to soften.

Boil the rice with a little salt for 15 minutes in 1½ litres (3 pints) of water. Cover the pan and simmer for 20 minutes. Leave to dry for 30 minutes after you have switched off the heat.

Meanwhile, peel and chop the onions finely and crush the garlic. Cut the tomatoes into small pieces. Chop the parsley, mint and pine nuts finely. When the rice is ready, thoroughly drain the vine leaves. Grease a very large saucepan with olive oil and line it with 2 or 3 vine leaves, to help prevent burning. Take all the vegetables, the garlic, pine nuts, herbs and spices, salt and pepper and mix thoroughly into the rice. Place the leaves on a board, vein side up. Take one leaf and place one full teaspoon of the rice mixture near the stem. Bring the two sides toward the middle and roll up into a small parcel. Gently squeeze. Place at the bottom of the saucepan, packing the rolled leaves close together. Continue doing this, making layers in the saucepan.

When you have finished, mix together the lemon juice, sugar, olive oil and about 250 ml (½ pint) of water. Pour over the vine leaves. If you like garlic, add extra slices of garlic in between the leaves. Place a plate on top of the leaves to stop them unrolling. Cover the saucepan and simmer for 2 hours. Check the level of the water every 30 minutes and add more if it looks low. Don't let the vine leaves dry out.

This dish can be eaten hot or cold. Serve hot with extra rice and a green salad.

For a cold dish, squeeze some fresh lemon juice over just before serving, and serve with a well-dressed tomato, basil and onion salad, black olives and pitta bread.

TOFU CHINESE STYLE WITH VEGETABLES

Tofu is soybean curd, considered in the Far East to have magic healing powers as well as nutritious ones. It is an inexpensive source of pure protein, containing many essential vitamins and minerals. You can buy it in many supermarkets and health food shops (it looks like a slab of thick, white cheese). For this recipe, buy the plain tofu not the smoked version. You should leave it in the marinade for several hours or, better still, overnight. Serve with boiled rice.

3 peppers (whatever colours you like)	1 tablespoon wine vinegar
3 onions	juice of 1 lemon
200 g (8 oz) mushrooms	1 teaspoon crushed ginger
2 cloves garlic	3 tablespoons olive oil (for the marinade)
500 g (1 lb) tofu	salt and freshly ground pepper
4 tablespoons shoyu sauce	olive oil for cooking
4 tablespoons tomato purée	3 teaspoons sunflower seeds

To marinate the tofu, chop it up into chunky bits and put in a bowl. Mix together the crushed garlic, shoyu sauce, tomato purée, wine vinegar, lemon juice, ginger, olive oil and salt and pepper, pour over the tofu and leave to marinate in the fridge, preferably overnight.

When you are ready to eat, prepare the vegetables and cut them into chunky slices. Carefully sieve all the marinade liquid into a bowl. Heat a few tablespoonfuls of olive oil and cook the vegetables and tofu for just a few minutes. Add the marinade for an extra 2 minutes. Line a grill-pan with foil and grill the sunflower seeds until lightly browned.

Serve with plain boiled rice and decorate with the toasted sunflower seeds.

VEGETABLE STROGANOFF

This is another dish I invented for unexpected visitors. It works well with almost any vegetable, depending on availability, but do avoid cabbage or Brussels sprouts which tend to over-dominate. Try mangetout, runner beans, stick beans, aubergine, fennel, or marrow.

500 g (1 lb) long grain rice
3 onions
200 g (8 oz) mushrooms
2 large peppers
3 leeks
4 large carrots
4 courgettes
1 clove garlic
olive oil

1 teaspoon parsley, chopped
1 teaspoon rosemary, chopped
1 small carton yoghourt
1 wine glass wine (red or white
  depending on your preference)
1 tablespoon wine vinegar
1 tablespoon shoyu sauce
salt and freshly ground pepper

Wash the rice thoroughly and add twice its volume in water. (Use a cup to make this easier to measure.) Bring to the boil and boil rapidly for 5 minutes. Reduce the heat, cover the pan and simmer for 30 minutes. The surface of the rice should now be pitted with little holes. If it is not dry and pitted, don't touch it or it will become starchy, but replace the lid and simmer for another 15 minutes. After you have finished cooking the rice, leave it for at least 30 minutes in the lidded pan to dry out (this also improves the taste).

Meanwhile, prepare and chop the vegetables and crush the garlic. Take a large deep saucepan, cover the base with a thin layer of olive oil and gently cook the vegetables for 5 minutes. Add the herbs for an extra minute. Add the yoghourt, wine, vinegar, shoyu sauce, salt and pepper. Mix well and simmer for 20 minutes. Taste the sauce and add extra wine and salt and pepper to taste. Serve the hot vegetables over the rice.

WINTER QUICHE

I make this quiche at least once a week in the winter. Served with a baked potato and a salad it makes an inexpensive, nutritious and tasty meal. It freezes well and can be prepared in advance.

Pastry
50 g (2 oz) butter or margarine
200 g (8 oz) wholemeal flour
salt
cold water

Filling
200 g (8 oz) courgettes, onions, mushrooms, peppers, leeks or tomatoes or a combination to your taste

olive oil
1 teaspoon thyme or marjoram, chopped
50 g (2 oz) Edam, Gruyère, Cheddar, Parmesan or Feta cheese, freshly grated
3 large eggs or 4 small eggs
salt and freshly ground pepper
6 tablespoons milk
½ teaspoon paprika or nutmeg

Rub the fat into the flour until it resembles breadcrumbs. Add a pinch of salt. Very slowly add 2 or 3 tablespoons of cold water until the mixture becomes a dough (I do all this in seconds in a food processor). Wrap in foil or clingfilm and leave in the fridge to rest for at least 30 minutes (this makes the dough easier to roll).

While the pastry is resting, prepare and slice the vegetables. Roll out the pastry into a flan dish and replace in the fridge so that it doesn't become limp. Sauté the vegetables in olive oil. When they are lightly browned, add the thyme or marjoram and continue cooking for an extra 2 minutes. Spread the mixture evenly over the pastry. Sprinkle the cheese over the vegetables. Whisk the eggs, salt, pepper and milk and pour evenly over the vegetables.

Sprinkle the paprika or nutmeg on top for colour. Place in a preheated oven, Gas Mark 4, 180°C, 350°F, for 45 minutes until golden brown.

Note:
The same method can be used for any vegetable that needs precooking such as spinach, broccoli, Brussels sprouts, cauliflower, parsnips, or Jerusalem artichokes. Simply boil the vegetables for the minimum period necessary to make them soft, drain very thoroughly and proceed as above.

WINTER WARMER CASSEROLE

I sometimes make this casserole on a Friday so that I do not have to cook on Saturday. You can use a variety of vegetables depending on what is available in the shops. I sometimes add broccoli, runner beans, mangetout, aubergine, cauliflower, celeriac or fennel (but don't add cabbage or Brussels sprouts as their tastes will dominate). You can leave it in the oven for several hours – it tastes better if it cooks slowly and has time for the flavours to blend. It freezes excellently.

200 g (8 oz) chick peas	olive oil
3 sticks celery	2 tablespoons parsley, chopped
4 carrots	coarsely
2 large onions	2 tablespoons coriander, chopped
3 large potatoes	coarsely
3 courgettes	4 tomatoes
3 parsnips	2 tablespoons yeast extract
2 turnips	salt and freshly ground pepper
1 swede	2 wine glasses dry white or red
2 cloves garlic	wine

Soak the chick peas in water overnight. Drain and rinse. Cover with fresh water and boil for 20 minutes. Drain. Prepare and chop all the vegetables except the tomatoes. Heat the olive oil and cook them gently with the garlic for 2–3 minutes in a casserole dish. Remove from the heat. Add the herbs, the whole tomatoes, the chick peas, the yeast extract and 1 litre (1½ pints) of water. Bring to the boil. Add salt and pepper, cover the dish and place in a low oven, Gas Mark 3, 170°C, 325°F, for 1½ hours. After 1 hour, gently stir in the wine and replace in the oven for a further 30 minutes. Adjust seasonings and serve boiling hot.

SALADS

I have not included a comprehensive section on salads because salad recipes are so readily available in other books. Also, because the main dishes we eat in winter are so filling I like to make accompanying salads light and simple, and so I have included only one or two basic salad recipes. I might also prefer occasionally to serve a cold vegetable dish, such as Leeks à la Grecque, instead of a salad; it sometimes seems more appropriate to a winter meal.

Remember that fresh salads should be prepared close to the meal and not dressed until the last moment. If you wish to make a salad before a special occasion, make it the night before and keep it totally airtight in the fridge. When you are catering for large numbers, always try to include some salads that can be prepared the day before your meal.

Many of the dishes in the starter section can be prepared as accompanying salads.

MIXED SALAD

This salad keeps well in the fridge, and is very colourful.

2 large cucumbers	6 sticks celery
2 green peppers	2 onions
1 red pepper	6 tomatoes
1 yellow pepper	8 tablespoons parsley

Cut the cucumbers, onions, tomatoes, peppers and celery into small cubes. Chop the parsley finely. Mix all the vegetables together. Serve with the following dressing.

VINAIGRETTE

8 tablespoons olive oil	1 teaspoon mustard powder
2 tablespoons white wine vinegar	1 teaspoon sugar
1 tablespoon lemon juice	salt and freshly ground pepper
1 clove garlic, crushed	(pinch of each)

Put all the ingredients into a lidded glass jar and shake carefully. I make this once a week and keep it in the jar in the fridge.

GREEN SALAD

In winter, some of the more colourful salad leaves are not available, but you can still make a delicious salad with just iceberg lettuce, onion and a few walnuts.

---

1 iceberg lettuce   100 g (4 oz) walnuts
2 onions

Wash and drain the iceberg lettuce thoroughly. Peel and cut the onion into thin rings. Chop the walnuts into quarters. Place the lettuce in a salad bowl, sprinkle the walnuts over and arrange the onion rings on top. Serve with a vinaigrette dressing. This salad can be prepared several hours before it is needed as long as you have thoroughly drained the leaves. Keep airtight and don't pour on the dressing until you are ready to eat.

TABBOULEH

Burghul (sometimes also called bulgar or cracked wheat) is available in many health food shops. It is very popular in the Middle East and Eastern Mediterranean countries where this salad is widely eaten.

1 tomato	6 tablespoons parsley
1 cucumber	2 tablespoons mint
200 g (8 oz) burghul	4 tablespoons olive oil
1 onion	juice of 2 lemons
	salt and freshly ground pepper

Chop the tomato and cucumber very finely. Salt generously and leave for 30 minutes. Pour boiling water over the burghul to just cover. Stir once and leave for 30 minutes.

Chop the onion, parsley and mint. Drain the burghul, which will have expanded, in a sieve. If too much moisture seems to be left, then squeeze it with your hand. Wash the salt off the tomatoes and cucumbers and drain thoroughly. Mix together the burghul, tomatoes, cucumbers, onion, parsley and mint thoroughly. Add the olive oil, lemon juice, salt and pepper and mix very well. Keep well covered and chill until used.

DESSERTS

Nowadays we are all health-conscious and there seems to be a trend away from eating desserts. Yet desserts do not need to be full of sugar and cream, although I have included a few here since they are deliciously irresistible and are fine to have occasionally. I like to serve large bowls of exotic fruits as well as one of the following desserts so that guests have a choice.

At dinner parties I wait for an hour or so after the main course before serving dessert. This allows the taste buds to rest, particularly after a heavy meal, and be ready to appreciate a new flavour and texture. A cold, light dessert is ideal after a hot meal.

Many of the following desserts take only seconds to prepare, so don't be tempted to omit a proper finale to your meal!

The Recipes

APPLE AND PISTACHIO FILO PASTRY

This is my variation of apple strudel, influenced by a love of pistachio nuts as used in Middle Eastern desserts. It can also be made with baklava pastry, but filo pastry (sometimes called strudel or phillo pastry) is much easier to obtain, frozen in many super-markets or fresh in many Greek shops. The recipe works well with very soft pears too. If you haven't used filo pastry before, then please read my notes under Mushrooms in Filo Pastry on page 107.

500 g (1 lb) packet filo pastry	200 g (8 oz) butter
8 large apples	200 g (8 oz) pistachio nuts
juice of 2 lemons	3 tablespoons brown sugar
6 tablespoons honey	2 tablespoons cinnamon
100 g (4 oz) sultanas	

You will also need:
   a rectangular ovenproof dish about 31 cm × 25 cm × 7 cm (12 in × 10 in × 3 in)
   a pastry brush

Remove the filo pastry from the freezer 1½–2 hours before you start cooking.

Peel and core the apples. Cut into large slices and sprinkle with half the lemon juice. Mix the honey with 125 ml (¼ pint) warm water. Soak the sultanas in hot water for 10 minutes.

Lay the filo pastry out flat. Melt half the butter. Brush the dish generously. Lay a sheet of filo across the base of the dish, leaving the ends to extend over the edge. Brush with butter. Continue overlapping the filo along one side of the dish, brushing each sheet generously with butter. When you have finished one side, do the same along the next side, brushing each sheet with butter. Continue in this way along each side until all the filo pastry has been used.

Drain the sultanas. Lay the apples, sultanas and pistachio nuts evenly over the filo base. Sprinkle with sugar, the remaining lemon juice and the cinnamon. Cut the remaining butter into several small pieces and dot over the apples. Pour over the honey and water mixture. Fold over the loose pieces of pastry, and brush each layer with butter. Brush the top layer with lots of butter. Cut through the layers of pastry in two or three places with a sharp knife; this allows some of the filling to come through and produces an attractive finish. Place in a preheated oven, Gas Mark 4, 180°C, 350°F, for 45 minutes until golden brown.

APPLE MERINGUE

A very delicious and simple dessert which freezes well. Vary the type of sugar for a slight variation in flavour.

1 packet digestive biscuits	6 large cooking apples
50 g (2 oz) margarine	juice of 1 lemon
4 eggs	150 g (6 oz) muscovado or any
1 tablespoon sherry or brandy	brown sugar

Keep the eggs at room temperature for 30 minutes before using. Blend or process the biscuits to smooth crumbs (or crush in a paper bag with a rolling pin). Melt the margarine and add the biscuit crumbs when slightly cool. Grease a pudding dish or flan dish and spread the biscuit mixture over the base. Press it down with a fork. Refrigerate until you have prepared the filling.

Separate the eggs. Add the sherry or brandy to the yolks. Peel and chop the apples and simmer gently in a small quantity of water. When soft, drain thoroughly and sprinkle with lemon juice. Add half the sugar. Mash with a fork or process to a smooth mixture. Add the egg yolks to the mixture, mix well and place over the biscuit base. Whisk the whites until very stiff. Slowly fold in the remaining sugar. Spread over the apple mixture and bake in a preheated oven, Gas Mark 4, 180°C, 350°F for 30 minutes until brown. Serve with cream or yoghourt.

Note:

To freeze this dish, bake for 30 minutes before you add the egg whites. Cool and freeze. When required, defrost thoroughly, add the meringue mixture and cook in the oven for 20 minutes at Gas Mark 4, 180°C, 350°F, until golden brown.

BAKED BANANAS IN LEMON AND RUM SAUCE

I often make this with bananas that have become a little soft. Served with cream, this makes a wonderful dinner party dessert. You can use Cointreau instead of rum if you prefer. It can be prepared early in the day, covered and left in the fridge until you start your meal. It is also very good cold!

2 eggs	2 tablespoons rum
100 g (4 oz) muscovado sugar	4 bananas
1½ teaspoons cornflour	100 g (4 oz) butter
juice of 1 lemon	pinch of nutmeg

Whisk the eggs and sugar until frothy, and gently fold in the sieved cornflour, the lemon juice and rum. Mix well. Slice the bananas thinly. Melt the butter in a frying pan and when it starts to froth, add the bananas and cook until lightly browned.

Lightly butter a shallow ovenproof dish. Arrange the bananas in the dish, cover with the rum and egg sauce, and sprinkle with nutmeg. Bake in a preheated oven, Gas Mark 4, 180°C, 350°F, for 25 minutes until brown. You can serve this with a drop of cream or yoghourt.

BROWN BREAD AND APPLE PUDDING

This is an old-fashioned, nursery pudding slightly updated, with an unusual toffee taste. I make it with different types of bread (black, wholemeal) and different types of brown sugar – try it with the muscovado dark brown sugar.

6 apples	3 tablespoons brown sugar
3 tablespoons sultanas	½ teaspoon cinnamon
6 slices brown or wholemeal bread (preferably a little stale)	3 eggs
	½ litre (1 pint) milk
butter or margarine to spread on the bread	½ teaspoon nutmeg

Peel and slice the apples. Place the sultanas in freshly boiled water for 10 minutes and then drain.

Butter an ovenproof dish. Spread the bread with the butter and lay 3 slices on the base. Cover with half the apples. Sprinkle with half the sultanas, sugar and cinnamon. Repeat these layers. Whisk the eggs and milk and pour this over the bread and apples. Sprinkle with nutmeg. Bake at Gas Mark 4, 180°C, 350°F, for about 50 minutes.

Serve very hot, with cream or yoghourt.

BROWNIES

I have included this recipe as a dessert as it really is excellent served with cream or yoghourt. I discovered this totally by chance when the dish I had planned to serve at a dinner party had not set (it happens to us all) and in desperation I cut up a brownie cake I had just made, poured on some rum and served it with cream. It was a great hit and I have included it here.

A traditional American brownie cake has a high sugar content, which I have reduced (giving a slightly less crusty-looking finish) but you can use more sugar if you prefer. Be sure to buy a good plain chocolate containing no milk or the brownies will be spoiled. Brownies freeze well or can be kept in an airtight container for up to six days.

---

200 g (8 oz) plain chocolate (such as Cadbury's Bournville, Terry's Dark, or one of the French cooking chocolates)
200 g (8 oz) butter or margarine
4 eggs
100 g (4 oz) muscovado or demerara sugar

100 g (4 oz) plain flour
2 teaspoons baking powder
½ teaspoon salt
200 g (8 oz) nuts (walnuts or pecans are traditionally used in brownies but almonds, hazelnuts, or any other combination will do)

Grease a large square cake tin and line with parchment paper. Break up the chocolate and cut up the butter and melt together in a pan or bowl over a saucepan of boiling water. (I use a frying pan over a saucepan.) Don't ever melt chocolate over a direct heat or it will go lumpy. Whisk together all the other ingredients and mix well with the slightly cooled butter–chocolate mixture.

Bake in a preheated oven, Gas Mark 4, 180°C, 350°F, for about 40 minutes. Press the cake lightly and if it springs back, then it is ready. If not, replace in the oven for another 10 minutes. Serve hot, cut into large pieces, with cream or yoghourt.

CHEESECAKE

It is a custom amongst Jewish families worldwide to eat dairy foods during the festival which celebrates the giving of the Law to Moses on Mount Sinai. This is a traditional recipe, more a dessert than a cake. When cooked it sets but is soft inside. It freezes very well and I often make it for parties in large quantities. It can be eaten as it is or with a large tablespoon of sour cream or Greek yoghourt.

200 g (8 oz) digestive biscuits	2 tablespoons sugar
100 g (4 oz) butter or margarine	juice of 1 lemon
500 g (1 lb) curd cheese	4 eggs

Blend or process the biscuits to smooth crumbs (or crush in a bag with a rolling pin). Melt the butter and mix in the biscuit mixture. Grease an ovenproof dish measuring about 30 cm × 25 cm (12 in × 10 in) and line with the crumbs, pressing down with a fork. Put in the fridge for 30 minutes.

Heat the oven to Gas Mark 4, 180°C, 350°F. Mix the cheese and sugar, add the lemon juice and then beat in the eggs. Pour over the crumb base, making sure it is smooth on top. Bake for 40 minutes. The cake should look brown on top and appear set. If you are in doubt, insert a knife. If the knife is dry when you take it out, the cake is ready. If wet, return to the oven for 10 minutes.

The taste of the cake improves if it is left for several hours or even overnight in the fridge after baking. You can eat it as it is or add the following topping, which you should make when you take the cake out of the oven.

Topping

150 ml (½ pint) carton sour cream or yoghourt	2 tablespoons sugar

Turn off the oven after taking out the cake. Mix together the sour cream or yoghourt and the sugar. Spread over the top of the cooked cake. Replace in the oven for 10 minutes (the oven will be hot enough from baking the cake). The topping will become very tasty if kept in the fridge for several hours after it has cooled.

CHESTNUT MOUSSE

I love chestnuts but I'm always surprised how many people don't like them, so I always make a fruit salad with lots of exotic fruits to accompany chestnut mousse. This mousse is simple to make, freezes well and can be prepared hours in advance. Sweetened chestnut purée in tins is widely available. If you find the sweetened chestnut purée in tins too sweet, buy a tin of whole chestnuts, mash them and add sugar to your taste.

4 tablespoons rum	6 eggs
4 tablespoons muscovado sugar	500 ml (1 pint) double cream
1 280 g (10 oz) tin chestnut purée	

Mash the chestnut purée and add the rum and sugar. Separate the eggs. Mix the yolks into the chestnut mixture. Whisk the egg whites until they are very stiff, and fold into the chestnut mixture. Whisk the cream until it has thickened. Fold gently into the chestnut mixture until it is fully absorbed. Transfer to an attractive bowl and leave in the fridge for several hours. I sometimes save a little of the cream for decoration.

CHOCOLATE MERINGUE

This is a great winter favourite with my family. I include it here for those miserable, wet days when you fancy eating something sweet! Buy a good plain chocolate that does not contain milk, such as Cadbury's Bournville, Terry's Dark Chocolate or Chocolat Menier. This is very important as some chocolates do not melt well.

1 packet digestive discuits	2 tablespoons liqueur (I use
100 g (4 oz) butter or margarine	Cointreau, but use your own
200 g (8 oz) plain chocolate	favourite)
6 eggs	6 tablespoons muscovado sugar

Crush the biscuits into crumbs. Melt the butter. Remove from the heat, add the crumbs and mix well. Take a pie dish (I use a quiche dish) and grease the base. Spread the biscuit mixture all over and pat down with a fork to make an even base. Put in the fridge for 30 minutes.

Break the chocolate into a pan or bowl and slowly melt over a saucepan of boiling water. (I use a frying pan over a saucepan.) Don't melt the chocolate over a direct heat or it will become lumpy. While the chocolate is melting, separate the eggs. Mix the liqueur with the egg yolks and add to the melted chocolate. Stir in thoroughly and pour over the biscuit base. Place in the fridge for 1 hour. Heat the oven to Gas Mark 4, 180°C, 350°F.

Whisk the egg whites until very stiff. Slowly add the sugar, beating well. Pour evenly over the chocolate and place in the oven until the meringue is browned. This will take approximately 15 minutes. Serve hot or cold.

CHOCOLATE MOUSSE

Chocolate mousse is a particularly popular sweet with all ages and is simple to make. It also freezes well. The secret of a good chocolate mousse, as with all chocolate cookery, is to use a good plain chocolate, not one containing milk. Use Cadbury's Bournville, Terry's Dark Chocolate or one of the French bitter chocolates such as Chocolat Menier. Chocolates containing milk or with a low cocoa butter content will not melt correctly and will spoil your finished dish. I have learnt this from bitter (!) experience after using own brand supermarket dark chocolate that ruined the mousse. . . .

4 eggs (at room temperature)	200 g (8 oz) plain chocolate
1 tablespoon brandy, rum or your favourite liqueur	

Separate the eggs. Mix the brandy or liqueur with the yolks. Break the chocolate into pieces and melt in a pan or bowl over a pan of boiling water. Whisk the egg whites until they are very stiff. When the chocolate has melted, remove from the heat, and add the yolk mixture with a wooden spoon. Gently fold in the stiff egg whites until fully mixed. Pour into a bowl with some room at the top for the mousse to expand. Cover completely and leave in the fridge for a few hours to set.

CHOCOLATE PUDDING CAKE

This is loved by children and adults alike (especially those of the male variety!), and freezes well. It must be kept cold as it doesn't taste as good at room temperature.

---

200 g (8 oz) butter
1 large packet muesli biscuits (if you don't like a crunchy taste use digestive or ginger biscuits)
200 g (8 oz) plain dark chocolate (Cadbury's Bournville, Terry's Dark, or a French dark chocolate)

50 g (2 oz) muscovado sugar
150 g (6 oz) chopped walnuts or almonds
3 eggs
2 tablespoons of your favourite liqueur

Remove the butter from the fridge 30 minutes before you start. Crush the biscuits to thick crumbs.

Melt the chocolate over a saucepan of boiling water (I put a frying pan over a large saucepan). Cream the butter and the sugar. Stir the nuts into the butter–sugar mixture and then add the biscuit crumbs. Separate the eggs. Stir the liqueur into the yolks. Whisk the egg whites until very stiff. As soon as the chocolate has melted, remove from the heat and add the egg yolks. Add this to the biscuit mixture. Gently fold in the stiff egg whites, checking carefully that no chocolate remains at the bottom of the dish.

Cover the dish and place in the fridge for several hours. Serve the pudding from the fridge with cream or yoghourt.

CRÈME BRÛLÉE

One of my favourite puddings, I find crème brûlée quite irresistible!

750 ml (1½ pints) double cream	6 eggs (use 4 whole eggs and
½ vanilla pod (vanilla essence can	2 yolks)
be used but is not as good)	1 tablespoon white sugar
	5 tablespoons muscovado sugar

Heat the cream with the vanilla pod. Remove from the heat just before the cream boils. In a heatproof bowl, beat the eggs (4 whole eggs and 2 yolks) and the white sugar. Remove the vanilla pod (it can be used again) and slowly add the cream to the eggs. Put the bowl over a saucepan of boiling water and very slowly stir until the mixture thickens. Do not allow it to boil. Remove from the heat and quickly place in an attractive ovenproof dish.

Cover with foil and refrigerate, preferably for a minimum of 12 hours (the crème brûlée improves if you prepare it the day before). Three hours before you are ready to eat the dessert, sprinkle the brown sugar thinly and evenly over the dish and place under a very hot grill, turning occasionally. Watch carefully until the sugar caramelises (it will start to change colour rapidly), and remove before it burns.

Replace in the fridge until the caramel becomes hard. When you are ready to serve, break the caramel in several pieces. Decadent!

CRÈME CARAMEL

Crème caramel makes a wonderful finish to a meal. Its only disadvantage is that it cannot be frozen. To make a classic crème caramel, use white sugar. I sometimes make it with muscovado sugar which produces an unusual toffee-type caramel.

150 g (6 oz) white sugar	1 vanilla pod
500 ml (1 pint) milk	3 eggs and 1 extra yolk

Grease a soufflé dish. Retain 2 tablespoons of the sugar and add the rest to 125 ml (¼ pint) of water. Heat slowly, stirring once or twice. When the sugar has started to dissolve and the water is boiling, watch carefully. The mixture will turn a golden brown. Remove immediately from the heat. Stir 2 tablespoons of water into the caramel and mix thoroughly. Quickly pour the mixture into the dish. Leave to cool.

Slowly warm the milk with the vanilla pod. Remove from the heat just before it starts to bubble. Whisk the eggs and add the remaining 2 tablespoons of sugar. Remove the vanilla pod from the milk and pour the milk on to the eggs. Whisk well, then pour over the caramel. Cover the dish with foil and place in a roasting tin in a preheated oven, Gas Mark 5, 190°C, 375°F. With a jug pour cold water into the roasting tin until it comes halfway up the dish. (I always do this when the dish is in the oven as I find it easier than carrying a heavy pan.) Bake for 40 minutes. The custard mixture will look set but not very firm. Remove from the oven and, when cool, cover and place in the fridge for several hours.

When you are ready to eat the crème caramel, take a serving dish or plate and very carefully cut around the rim of the crème caramel with a knife. Place the serving dish on top and quickly turn both dishes over. The caramel will slowly move to the serving plate, and you can pour the sauce over the top. If there is a lot of caramel stuck to the dish, stand the dish in a roasting pan of freshly boiled water for a few minutes and it will soften. Serve with cream.

DATE DELIGHT

This simple dessert is best made with fresh dates, but, if these are not available, dried dates can be used.

100 g (4 oz) raisins	100 g (4 oz) clear thin honey
500 g (1 lb) dates	100 g (4 oz) chopped hazelnuts
6 tablespoons sherry (or your favourite liqueur)	125 ml (¼ pint) single cream or yoghourt

Soak the raisins in boiling water for 5 minutes and drain thoroughly. Stone the dates and chop into quarters. Mix the sherry and honey with 2 tablespoons of water. Put the dates and the raisins in a deep bowl, pour over the honey and sherry mixture, mix well and cover the bowl. Make sure all the dates and raisins are covered with the liquid. Place in the fridge for a minimum of 1 hour.

Sprinkle the nuts and cream or yoghourt on top just before serving.

FIGS, YOGHOURT AND NUTS

This takes only seconds to prepare and can be made at the last minute with ingredients to hand for any unexpected guests. Do use fresh figs if you have them.

500 g (1 lb) dried figs	250 ml (½ pint) carton
10 tablespoons Cointreau or	Greek-style yoghourt
Courvoisier	100 g (4 oz) chopped nuts
	(walnuts or almonds are best)

Soak the figs for a minimum of 30 minutes (or if they appear very dry, a couple of hours) in the Cointreau or Courvoisier. Spoon over the yoghourt and nuts. Easy and tasty!

GINGER CHESTNUT PUDDING

12 ginger biscuits
200 g (8 oz) plain dark chocolate
250 ml (½ pint) double cream
1 tin chestnut purée

100 g (4 oz) chopped walnuts
100 g (4 oz) brown sugar
  (muscovado or demerara)
4 tablespoons brandy

Crush the ginger biscuits to crumbs. Melt the chocolate over a pan of boiling water (I put it in a frying pan over a saucepan). Whisk the cream until it is very thick. Drain the chestnut purée of any liquid and mix with the biscuit crumbs, walnuts and the sugar until it is smooth. Add the melted chocolate and the brandy. Fold in the whipped cream slowly. Pour into a serving dish and leave in the fridge to set for a few hours. You might like to save some chocolate and cream to decorate.

GRAPES AND KIWI BRÛLÉE

This dessert can be made throughout the year using seasonal fruit, and works excellently with any soft fruit. The combination of kiwi fruit and grapes is particularly delicious. Use green, seedless grapes and slightly soft kiwis. Other unusual fruits to try are mango, guava, passion fruit and melon, either singly or in combination. Experiment, too, with different sugars, brown ones giving a more nutty taste.

500 g (1 lb) grapes	250 ml (½ pint) double cream
3 kiwi fruits	150 g (6 oz) sugar
2 wine glasses dry white wine	

Remove the stalks of the grapes. Peel and slice the kiwi fruits into thin slices. Arrange the grapes and kiwi slices in a heatproof dish and pour over the wine. Cover and leave to stand in the fridge for several hours.

When you are ready to eat, pour the cream over the fruit and sprinkle the sugar evenly on top. Place under a very hot grill for a few minutes. You will see the sugar caramelise as the cream starts to bubble. Eat immediately. (It can also be made in advance, refrigerated, and served cold.)

GUAVA, GRAPE AND MANGO DELIGHT

This is quick to make and has an unusual blend of tastes. Prepare no more than two hours in advance as the grapes can become mushy.

1 large fresh mango	200 g (8 oz) seedless grapes
1 large fresh guava	6 tablespoons dry white wine

Remove the skin from the mango and guava and slice thickly. Wash and dry the grapes. Place all the fruit into a bowl and pour the wine over. Keep airtight in the fridge until you are ready to eat. Serve with whipped cream or yoghourt.

HONEY CAKE

This is an adaptation of a traditional Jewish honey cake which is eaten at the New Year to bring sweetness for the forthcoming year. It is a great favourite as a cake, but is equally successful as a dessert with cream or yoghourt.

The taste improves after a few days as the cake becomes stickier. It keeps for a couple of weeks in an airtight tin and freezes well.

250 g (10 oz) thin, clear honey	100 g (4 oz) demerara sugar
300 g (12 oz) self-raising flour	4 tablespoons olive oil
1 teaspoon ground ginger	125 ml (¼ pint) warm water
1 teaspoon mixed spice	100 g (4 oz) almonds (halved)
3 eggs	1 tablespoon sherry

Bring a saucepan of water to the boil then remove from the heat. Warm the honey, still in its jar or bowl, in the hot water for 5 minutes.

Mix together the flour, ginger and mixed spice. In another bowl, whisk together the eggs and sugar and add the honey and the oil. Add the warm water and the dry ingredients gradually, stirring constantly. When fully mixed, pour into a large baking dish, measuring about 25 cm × 31 cm × 7 cm (10 in × 12 in × 3 in), and dot with the almonds. Bake in a preheated oven, Gas Mark 4, 180°C, 350°F, for 1 hour until golden brown. Make some small holes in the cake and pour in the sherry, then serve hot with cream or yoghourt.

HOT GRAPEFRUIT

2 grapefruit	1 tablespoon cinnamon
2 teaspoons muscovado or demerara sugar	

Halve the grapefruit, cut around the rim and separate the segments. Spread the sugar over the grapefruit. Sprinkle the cinnamon on top and put under the grill at its lowest setting. Watch carefully until the sugar melts completely. Eat immediately.

KIWI, ORANGE AND GRAPES CARAMEL IN CREAM

After a hard day at work this is a quick dessert to make for last-minute guests. If fresh lychees, sharon fruit or passion fruit are available, add these too.

3 large oranges
3 kiwi fruits
200 g (8 oz) seedless grapes
150 g (6 oz) muscovado sugar

2 tablespoons rum
300 ml (10 fl oz) double cream or yoghourt

Peel the oranges and kiwi and remove the stalks from the grapes.

Place the sugar in a small saucepan with 125 ml (¼ pint) of water and bring to the boil; stir it as soon as the liquid starts to boil. Watch carefully, and as soon as the mixture turns to a dark brown, slowly add a little more water (about 8 tablespoons). Stir thoroughly and gently heat until the sauce is smooth. Line a bowl with this caramel and arrange the prepared fruit over. Pour the rum over the fruit, cover with foil and place in the fridge. When you are ready to eat, whisk the cream or yoghourt and pour over the fruit.

KIWI PAVLOVA

My Australian sister-in-law Dianne's pavlova tastes much better than any other I have ever eaten, perhaps because it is made in a rather unusual way. She always has to make several for parties as they disappear at a very fast rate. Make this when you are in a very relaxed mood as it is fragile!

4 egg whites (chilled)
200 g (8 oz) castor sugar
pinch of salt
2 level teaspoons cornflour
1 teaspoon white wine vinegar
1 teaspoon vanilla essence (or if you prefer, boil a vanilla pod for 20 minutes, sieve the liquid and use 1 cooled teaspoon)

300 ml (10 fl oz) whipping cream
2 kiwi fruit or passion fruit or any other soft fruit in season
50 g (2 oz) dark chocolate, grated (optional, for decoration)

You will need a 25 cm (10 in) dinner plate which is slightly convex in which to cook the pavlova. Line the plate with baking parchment or rice paper. If these aren't available, butter the plate and sprinkle water over it. Heat the oven to Gas Mark 2, 150°C, 300°F. Make room on the top shelf for the plate and the pavlova mixture.

Take the eggs out of the fridge only when you are ready to start cooking (the ingredients and equipment must remain cool). Mix the sugar, pinch of salt and cornflour. Whisk the egg whites with the cornflour mixture until they form stiff, glossy peaks. This will take 5 minutes with an electric mixer.

Mix the vinegar and vanilla essence into the mixture and then whisk. Spread this over the plate and pile it high. Smooth the top. Gently place it at the top of the preheated oven (try to make sure you don't knock it against the oven shelf). Bake for 1 hour and don't open the oven door while it is cooking.

At the end of the hour, turn off the heat and leave the pavlova in the oven undisturbed (don't even open the door) for several hours to dry out. You can leave it overnight if you wish or make it in the morning and leave all day.

When required, whisk the cream and pile it all over the top. Peel and thinly slice the fruit and dot over the cream. It is customary to use passion or kiwi fruit, but different-coloured soft fruits also look very pretty. You might like to grate bitter chocolate on top.

MANGO FOOL

I adore fresh mango. Normally I don't like to cook such a lovely fruit, but when there is an abundance of fresh fruit this recipe becomes useful. It can be made with double cream or yoghourt, and it works equally well with pears, apples, guava and pineapple.

3 mangoes	2 tablespoons cornflour
2 wine glasses dry white wine	1 egg
2 tablespoons thin honey	6 tablespoons Greek yoghourt or
3 tablespoons cinnamon	double cream
juice of 1 lemon	

Skin the mangoes and place the flesh in a saucepan together with the white wine, honey, cinnamon and lemon juice. Gently simmer for 20 minutes. Watch carefully that the liquid does not boil. If it starts to boil, add some extra wine and a couple of tablespoons of water. Strain the juice into a bowl and transfer the mangoes to a dish.

Stir a few tablespoons of water into the cornflour to make a thick, smooth paste. Use only the egg yolk of the egg and mix it with the yoghourt or cream, cornflour paste and the mango juice. Simmer this mixture in a saucepan until it begins to boil and become thick.

Pour over the mangoes, cover, and leave to set for several hours in the fridge.

MELON WITH PORT

This simple melon dish can also be served as a starter. I like to use
Galia, Ogen or Cantaloup melons.

2 melons
port

Place the melons in the fridge for several hours, then cut in half.
Remove all the seeds. Pour a generous amount of port into the
hollow of each half and leave in the fridge for at least 1 hour for the
melon to absorb the taste of the port.

ORANGES IN CARAMEL

This is popular in restaurants on the desserts trolley. I like to use the large Jaffa oranges, and brown sugar for the caramel.

4 large oranges	150 g (6 oz) sugar
4 tablespoons Cointreau	

Peel the oranges and remove the rind and pith. Do this over a bowl to catch the juice. Save a little of the peel and chop it into very thin slices. Slightly open the oranges, partially separate each segment and place in a large dish. Generously sprinkle the Cointreau over the oranges.

Place the sugar and 125 ml (¼ pint) of water in a fairly large saucepan and very slowly bring to the boil. As soon as the water has started to steam, stir so that the sugar dissolves evenly. When the sugar and water becomes a dark golden caramel, remove immediately from the heat (it will be very hot so be careful you do not burn yourself). Slowly pour in a further 125 ml (¼ pint) of water, stirring with a wooden spoon. If the caramel sauce becomes lumpy, put back on a gentle heat for a few seconds and stir until smooth. Pour this sauce over the oranges. Add the sliced orange peel to the remains of the sauce in the pan and allow to cook for a minute. Use to decorate the oranges. Chill.

ORANGE MOUSSE

Italian amaretti biscuits, a type of macaroon, make an excellent base in dessert dishes. In this recipe, I soak them in Cointreau for its orange flavour. The mousse does take time to prepare, but is well worth it, and it freezes well.

---

200 g (8 oz) amaretti biscuits
3 tablespoons Cointreau (or your
favourite liqueur)
4 eggs and 2 extra yolks
100 g (4 oz) muscovado sugar

250 ml (½ pint) double cream
juice of 3 oranges
50 g (2 oz) plain chocolate, grated
(optional, for decoration)

Crush the amaretti. Butter a large soufflé dish and line the base with the crushed biscuits. Sprinkle with the Cointreau. Mix the 4 eggs, the yolks, and sugar in a bowl over a saucepan of simmering water (removed from the heat). Whisk the mixture until it becomes thick and continue to whisk for another couple of minutes, but do not allow it to boil.

In another bowl, whisk the cream until it thickens. Gently fold the cream and the orange juice into the egg mixture. Pour over the amaretti base and place in the fridge for several hours.

You may like to decorate with grated plain chocolate, pieces of orange and whipped cream.

PASSION FRUIT MERINGUE

This dessert can be made with a variety of fillings. I like to use passion fruit but try kiwi, sharon fruit, mango or guava.

1 packet digestive or gingernut biscuits	6 passion fruit (if they're very small, use 8)
100 g (4 oz) butter or margarine	200g (4 oz) muscovado sugar
4 egg whites	

Heat the oven to Gas Mark 3, 160°C, 325°F. Crush the biscuits into crumbs in a bag with a rolling pin or in a food processor. Melt the butter and mix in the biscuit crumbs. Butter an ovenproof pie dish and press the biscuit mixture all around the base until it forms a thin covering. Place the dish in the fridge.

Whisk the egg whites until very stiff. Halve the passion fruits and scrape all the flesh with a teaspoon into a bowl. Pour over the biscuit base. Fold the sugar into the stiffly beaten egg whites and gently spread the meringue over the passion fruits. Smooth the top and place it immediately in the oven for approximately 35 minutes until lightly browned.

PECAN PIE

This is a sticky pie, loved by all children and adults with a sweet tooth, although the sugar content is low. It keeps for days in an airtight tin.

75 g (3 oz) butter or margarine	2 tablespoons honey
10 digestive biscuits	1 teaspoon cinnamon
3 eggs	200 g (8 oz) pecan nuts (or
2 tablespoons olive oil	walnuts)
2 tablespoons brown sugar	1 teaspoon nutmeg
2 tablespoons orange juice	

Melt the butter or margarine. Crush the biscuits to crumb consistency in a food processor or with a rolling pin, and mix into the butter. Spread the mixture over the base of a pie dish. Put in the fridge to keep cool (otherwise it will become sticky).

Whisk the eggs, oil, sugar, orange juice, honey and cinnamon. Halve the pecans and arrange them over the base of the pie. Pour the egg mixture over, and sprinkle with nutmeg. Place in a preheated oven, Gas Mark 4, 180°C, 350°F, for 45 minutes until golden brown. Serve with yoghourt or cream.

PINEAPPLE IN RUM

Often the simplest and seemingly most obvious combinations make a perfect dessert, particularly after a large meal.

2 pineapples	whipping cream or yoghourt
8 tablespoons rum	

Cut the pineapples in half lengthways. Cut out the pineapple flesh with a sharp knife and reserve the shells in the fridge. Chop the flesh into small cubes and place in a bowl. Pour the rum over and store in an airtight container in the fridge until you are ready to eat. To serve, pile the cubes and juice into the shells, whip some cream and place a small amount on top.

SYLLABUS

This is a variation of an old English pudding, especially delicious on cold, wet, winter nights. Prepare it several hours before, if possible, to allow the flavours to blend.

300 ml (10 fl oz) double cream	6 tablespoons sherry, rum or
2 tablespoons brown sugar	Cointreau, or any other liqueur
	to your taste
	juice of 1 lemon

Whip the cream until it is very thick. Slowly add the sugar, liqueur and lemon, and whisk until fully blended. Place immediately in the refrigerator for a minimum of 6 hours.

WINTER FRUIT SALAD

This is a delicious and refreshing end to a meal. You can vary the fruit depending on availability and price, but try to choose at least six different fruits for a colourful mixture and a variety of flavours. Try passion fruit, lychees, fresh dates, fresh figs, papayas (papaw) and any citrus fruit.

1 Galia melon	2 sharon fruit
1 pineapple	2 star fruit (carambola)
1 mango	juice of 2 lemons
1 guava	2 wine glasses white wine
3 kiwi fruit	

Cut the melon in half, remove the seeds and scoop out the fruit. Cut into medium-sized chunks. Do the same with the pineapple, mango and guava. Peel the kiwis, sharon and star fruits and cut into thin slices. Mix the fruit thoroughly and stir in the lemon juice. Place in the fridge in an airtight container. One hour before your meal, mix in the white wine and return to the fridge. You might like to serve this dish with single cream or yoghourt.

YOGHOURT AND HONEY

A deceptively simple dessert, that I nearly didn't include.

150 g (6 oz) pistachio nuts	8 tablespoons clear thin honey
300 ml (10 fl oz) Greek yoghourt	

Halve the pistachio nuts. Pour the yoghourt into individual dishes (I like to use small ramekins). Dribble 2 tablespoons of honey over each serving, and sprinkle with pistachios. Serve immediately.

ENTERTAINING

Many of my childhood memories are of my extended family eating around a large table. Festivals were celebrated with large, cheerful meals, and all hospitality centred around eating. I still find that sharing meals with friends and family is one of the most pleasant ways of spending time together. But there is nothing worse than spending the whole day cooking and being too tired to enjoy your guests' company. You do not have to be a Superman/woman. Plan the meal carefully and cook and/or freeze some of the dishes in advance. If you don't have a lot of time, choose dishes that can be prepared quickly. Consider the meal as a whole and vary textures, hot and cold, colour, etc., and avoid too many filling, heavy dishes in one meal.

I like to plan menus with an ethnic or geographical theme, such as Middle Eastern Style below. I found this helpful when I first started cooking vegetarian meals as I found it difficult to plan meals. But I also like to be flexible – you don't have to stick rigidly to one theme. The menus below offer alternatives; cook as few or as many dishes as you like!

1 Middle Eastern Style (A)

Ful Medames / Hamin Eggs / Fried Aubergine / Tahini Dip
served with pitta bread, olives (black, green and garlic) and
pickled cucumber

Couscous and Vegetables, Mixed Salad

Apple and Pistachio Filo Pastry / Yoghourt and Honey / Date
Delight, Greek yoghourt or cream

2 Middle Eastern Style (B)

Aubergine Middle Eastern Style / Avocado and Pepper Spread /
Feta and Salad served with pitta bread, olives, chillis and
cucumber

Okra and Tomato Pilaf, rice, Green Salad and Leeks in Tomato
and Garlic Sauce

Mango Fool / Figs, Yoghourt and Nuts / Crème Caramel

3 Italian Style (A)

Artichoke Hearts in Garlic / Cream of Courgette Soup

Pasta and Pepper Sauce, Green Salad and Mushroom and Garlic
Starter

Chocolate Pudding Cake / Crème Caramel / Melon with Port

4 Italian Style (B)

Stuffed Mushrooms

Chick Pea Pasta, Green Salad, mangetout, carrots and onion
(sautéd in olive oil with oregano and then steamed for ten
minutes)

Oranges in Caramel / Crème Brûlée / Kiwi, Orange and Grapes
Caramel in Cream

5 Greek Style (A)

Halumi Cheese and Egg / Aubergine and Tahini Spread / Hummus, pitta bread, pickled cucumbers and olives (green, black and garlic)

Stuffed Aubergines / Stuffed Vine Leaves, rice or Tabbouleh and Mixed Salad

Figs, Yoghourt and Nuts / Pineapple in Rum / Ginger Chestnut Pudding

6 Greek Style (B)

Feta and Salad / Fried Aubergine / Lentil and Tahini Dip, pitta bread, cucumber and olives (black, green and garlic)

Spanakopitta (Spinach and Feta in Filo Pastry), rice, Mixed Salad, Spinach and Cream

Date Delight / Melon with Port / Chocolate Meringue

7 Winter Warmer (Western European) Style

Pumpkin Starter

Winter Warmer Soup

Cashew Nut, Vegetable and Cheese Flan, baked potatoes, Savoury Tomatoes, Green Salad

Chocolate Mousse / Passion Fruit Meringue / Winter Fruit Salad

8 Eastern European (Jewish) Style

Egg and Onion, rye bread

Barley and Vegetable Soup

Winter Warmer Casserole served with extra vegetables from the recipe, new potatoes and Green Salad

Honey Cake / Cheesecake / Pineapple in Rum

9 *English Vegetarian Style (A)*

Spinach and Cream, granary bread

Parsnip and Onion Soufflé, baked potatoes, Green Salad, Stuffed
Onions

Apple Meringue / Oranges in Caramel / Syllabub

10 *English Vegetarian Style (B)*

Turnips in Garlic and Breadcrumbs

Cream of Courgette Soup

Mushroom and Curd Cheese Marjoram Pie, new potatoes, Mixed
Salad, Mushroom and Garlic Starter

Chocolate Mousse / Winter Fruit Salad / Crème Brûlée

11 *French Style*

Grilled Goat's Cheese

Mushroom and Garlic Soup

Stuffed Artichokes, Turnips in Garlic and Breadcrumbs, Leeks à
la Grecque, Green Salad

Chestnut Mousse / Crème Brûlée / Passion Fruit Meringue

Parties

Cocktails

Aubergine Middle Eastern Style
Avocado Dip
Avocado and Pepper Spread
Hamin Eggs
Pumpkin Starter
Spinach and Cream
Brussels Sprouts Pâté
Ful Medames

Tahini Dip
Leeks à la Grecque
Watercress Eggs
Winter Vegetable Hors d'Oeuvre / Vegetable Antipasto with
Aioli, pitta bread, pickled cucumbers, olives (green, black, garlic)

Buffet Meals

1 Avocado, Hummus, Aubergine Middle Eastern Style Dips
   Winter Vegetable Hors d'Oeuvre
   Pumpkin Cream Soup
   Mushroom Stroganoff
   Hazelnut and Vegetable Pilaf
   Stuffed Mushrooms
   Savoury Tomatoes / bowls of Mixed, Green and Tabbouleh
   Salads

   Chocolate Mousse / Passion Fruit Meringue / Pineapple in
   Rum

2 Artichoke Hearts in Garlic
   Aubergine Middle Eastern Style
   Mushrooms in Filo Pastry
   Stuffed Mushrooms
   Leeks in Tomato and Garlic Sauce
   Platters of Watercress Eggs, Vegetable Antipasto with Aioli,
   Green Salad

   Chocolate Meringue / Ginger Chestnut Pudding / Winter Fruit
   Salad

3 Winter Vegetable Hors d'Oeuvre
   Fried Aubergine Slices
   Stuffed Courgettes
   Spanakopitta (Spinach and Feta in Filo Pastry)
   Bowls of Tabbouleh / Green Salad / Hummus / Tahini Dip
   Pitta bread, olives, cucumber

   Baked Bananas in Lemon and Rum Sauce / Melon with Port /
   Brownies with cream or yoghourt

Christmas and festive occasions

For festive occasions, choose dishes that can be prepared in
advance, so that you can enjoy the day. I have suggested two
menus where most of the courses can be made in advance and

frozen. The starters and fruit salad can be prepared the day before your meal (add lots of lemon juice to the fruit salad) and kept in the fridge in airtight containers. You then need only prepare the salads on the day.

The buffet menus above are also suitable for festive occasions. Do have breaks in between the courses and, if you feel very full after the main course, wait an hour or so before serving dessert. For special occasions I like to offer a lot of choice so the following menus are rather large. You need not make every dish on these menus if you don't want to!

1 Avocado Dip, Aubergine Middle Eastern Style, Tahini Dip and Hummus served with cucumbers, olives and pitta bread

Watercress and Wine Soup (make this when you see the watercress as it is often not available the week before Christmas)
Cream of Parsnip Soup

Spanakopitta (Spinach and Feta in Filo Pastry), Stuffed Aubergines, Courgettes or Peppers
Make extra rice and serve with mangetout, courgettes, and onions and thyme sautéd for five minutes, then add a cup of water and steam for ten minutes.
Salads: Green Salad, Leeks à la Grecque, Tabbouleh

Baked Bananas in Lemon and Rum Sauce / Winter Fruit Salad / Chocolate Pudding Cake with cream or yoghourt

2 Artichoke hearts in Garlic / Brussels Sprouts Pâté, rye bread

Avocado Soup
Pumpkin Cream Soup (buy the pumpkin several weeks before Christmas as it is often in short supply in December)

Mushroom Stroganoff / Lentils with Vegetables (prepare the vegetables for the lentil dish and make extra to be served as an accompanying dish)
Salads: Mixed Salad / Mushroom and Garlic Starter / Green Salad

Apple and Pistachio Filo Pastry / Grapes and Kiwi Brûlée / Melon with Port, cream or yoghourt.

BIBLIOGRAPHY

I was married in Jerusalem in 1972 and as a wedding present I received Claudia Roden's *A Book of Middle Eastern Food*. At the time, I lived on cottage cheese and omelettes as I wanted to be a vegetarian. I embarked on the book with great enthusiasm, cooking vast Middle Eastern vegetarian meals for my husband John and numerous friends who always seemed to eat with us. In truth, this was a reaction to the awful meat dishes that the Australian (and then very) carnivorous John and his flatmates used to cook in huge quantities. So, Claudia Roden's wonderful book has ever since been a great favourite of mine. It taught me to cook marvellous Mediterranean and Middle Eastern dishes, introduced me to new combinations of vegetables, herbs and spices and led me on the path to write this book. It is also a good read and I highly recommend it.

Jane Grigson's books are marvellous; they are very readable, informative and full of interesting tales. I would also recommend that you borrow Elizabeth David's books from the library. They do have very interesting sections on vegetables but look at them before you buy as large sections of her books cover meat, poultry and fish. The other books listed are all ones that I have enjoyed and found useful. The Mollie Katzen books are published in the USA but can be bought here.

Elizabeth David *A Book of Mediterranean Food*, Penguin Books, London, 1955
Elizabeth David *French Provincial Cooking*, Penguin Books, London, 1964
Elizabeth David *Italian Food*, Penguin Books, London, 1963
Jane Grigson's *Fruit Book*, Penguin Books, London, 1983
Jane Grigson's *Vegetable Book*, Penguin Books, London, 1980
Marcella Hazan *Marcella's Kitchen*, Papermac, 1988
Marcella Hazan *The Classic Italian Cookbook*, Papermac, 1981
Mollie Katzen *The Enchanted Broccoli Forest*, Ten Speed Press, Berkeley, California, 1982
Mollie Katzen *Moosewood Cookbook*, Ten Speed Press, Berkeley, California, 1977

Rosamond Man *The Complete Meze Table*, Ebury Press, London, 1986

Claudia Roden *A Book of Middle Eastern Food*, Penguin Books, London, 1968

Claudia Roden *Mediterranean Cookery*, BBC Books, London, 1987

Anna Thomas *The Vegetarian Epicure*, Penguin Books, London, 1973

INDEX

aioli, 47–8, 175

apple: apple fool, 159; apple meringue, 139, 174; apple and pistachio filo pastry, 137–8, 172, 176; brown bread and apple pudding, 141

artichoke: artichoke hearts in garlic, 19, 172, 175, 176; artichokes in butter and lemon sauce, 17–18; stuffed artichokes, 120, 174

artichoke, Jerusalem: Jerusalem artichoke soup, 67

aubergine: aubergine Middle Eastern style, 20, 172, 174, 175, 176; aubergine with tahini, 20, 122; aubergine and tahini spread, 122, 173; baked aubergine and tomato, 89–90; fried aubergine slices, 30, 172, 173, 175; preparing, 20, 121; stuffed aubergines, 121–2, 173, 176

avocado, 6; avocado dip, 21, 174, 175, 176; avocado and pepper spread, 23, 172, 174; avocado soup, 55, 176; avocado vinaigrette, 24; growing from stone, 6; ripening, 6, 24; testing for ripeness, 6, 24

bamia, *see* okra

banana: baked bananas in lemon and rum sauce, 140, 175, 176; banana and nut pilaf, 91–2

barley and vegetable soup, 56, 173

beans: bean soup, 57; beans Egyptian style, 31; ful medames, 31, 172, 174; haricot bean soup, 66; pasta and bean soup, 72; white bean soup, 83; winter warmer soup, 85

blender, 8

bread: brown bread and apple pudding, 141; croûtons, 71

broccoli: broccoli and cheese bake, 93; broccoli pâté, 25; broccoli soup, 58

brownies, 142, 175

Brussels sprouts: Brussels sprouts and garlic soup, 59; Brussels sprouts pâté, 25, 174, 176

buckwheat and vegetable pilaf, 94

bulgar, *see* burghul

burghul: pumpkin and burghul pie, 116; tabbouleh, 134, 173, 175, 176

butter and lemon sauce, 17

carambola: winter fruit salad, 167, 173, 174, 175, 176

carrots à la grecque, 36

cashew nut, vegetable and cheese flan, 95, 173

cauliflower soup, 60

celeriac: celeriac in lemon sauce, 26; celeriac soup, 61; peeling, 26

cheese: broccoli and cheese bake, 93; cashew nut, vegetable and cheese flan, 95, 173; cheesecake, 143–4; fennel delight, 100; Feta and salad, 29, 172; grilled goat's cheese, 33, 174; halumi cheese and egg, 34, 172; mushroom and curd cheese marjoram pie, 106, 174; mushrooms in filo pastry, 107–8; spinach and Feta in filo pastry, 118–19

cheesecake, 143–4, 173

chestnuts: chestnut casserole, 96; chestnut mousse, 145, 174; ginger chestnut pudding, 153, 175

chick peas: chick pea pasta, 97, 172; hummus, 35

chocolate, 7; chocolate meringue, 146, 173, 175; chocolate mousse, 147, 173, 174, 175; chocolate pudding cake, 148, 172, 176; melting, 146, 147

coriander, 4

courgettes: courgette pâté, 25; courgette and tomato soup, 62; courgettes à la Grecque, 36; courgettes and mushrooms in sour cream, 27; cream of courgette soup, 63, 172, 174; stuffed courgettes, 121–2, 175, 176

couscous and vegetables, 98, 172

cracked wheat, *see* burghul

cream, 5; crème brûlée, 149, 172, 174; kiwi, orange and grapes caramel in cream, 156; syllabub, 166, 174

crème brûlée, 149, 172, 174

crème caramel, 150, 172

croustade, leeks, 102

croûtons, 71

cutting boards, 9–10

date delight, 151, 172, 173

desserts, 135–68: apple meringue, 139; apple and pistachio filo pastry, 137–8, 172; baked bananas in

desserts – *cont.*
lemon and rum sauce, 140, 175, 176; brown bread and apple pudding, 141; brownies, 142, 175; cheesecake, 143–4, 173; chestnut mousse, 145, 174; chocolate meringue, 146, 173, 175; chocolate mousse, 147, 173, 174, 175; chocolate pudding cake, 148, 172, 176; crème brûlée, 149, 172, 174; crème caramel, 150, 172; date delight, 151, 172, 173; figs, yoghourt and nuts, 144, 172; ginger chestnut pudding, 153, 175; grapes and kiwi brûlée, 153, 176; guava, grape and mango delight, 154; honey cake, 155, 173; hot grapefruit, 157; kiwi, orange and grapes caramel in cream, 156, 172; kiwi pavlova, 157–8; mango fool, 159, 172; melon with Port, 160, 172, 176; orange mousse, 162; oranges in caramel, 161, 172, 174; passion fruit meringue, 163, 173; pecan pie, 164; pineapple in rum, 165, 173, 175; syllabub, 166, 174; winter fruit salad, 167, 173, 174, 175, 176; yoghourt and honey, 168, 172
dips: aubergine and tahini spread, 122, 173; avocado dip, 21, 174, 175, 176; avocado and pepper spread, 23, 172, 174; lentil and tahini dip, 38, 173; tahini dip, 45, 172, 174; winter vegetable dips, 50

eggplant, *see* aubergine
eggs: chestnut mousse, 145, 174; chocolate meringue, 146, 173, 175; chocolate mousse, 147, 173, 174, 175; crème brûlée, 149, 172, 174; crème caramel, 150, 172; egg and onion, 28, 173; halumi cheese and egg, 34, 173; hamin eggs, 31–2, 172, 174; kiwi pavlova, 157–8; mayonnaise, 21–2; orange mousse, 162; passion fruit meringue, 163, 173, 174, 175; watercress eggs, 49, 175
entertaining, 169; menus, 170–4
equipment, 8–10

fennel delight, 100
Feta cheese, *see* cheese
figs, yoghourt and nuts, 144, 172
filo pastry, 6, 107; apple and pistachio filo pastry, 137–8, 172, 176; mushrooms in filo pastry, 107–8, 175; Spanakopitta, 118–19, 175

flans and pies: cashew nut, vegetable and cheese flan, 95, 173; fennel delight, 100; leeks croustade, 102; mushroom and curd cheese marjoram pie, 106; pecan pie, 164; pumpkin and burghul pie, 116; pumpkin pie, 115; winter quiche, 128–9
food processor, 8
fool, apple, 159; guava, 159; mango, 159; pear, 159; pineapple, 159
fruit. See also apple, banana, etc: Winter fruit salad, 167, 173, 174, 175, 176
ful medames, 31, 172, 174

garlic: artichoke hearts in garlic, 19, 172, 175, 176; Brussels sprouts and garlic soup, 59; garlic sauce, 48; leeks in tomato and garlic sauce, 37, 172, 175; mushroom and garlic soup, 70, 174; mushroom and garlic starter, 39, 172, 174, 176; turnips in garlic and breadcrumbs, 46, 174
garlic press, 10
ginger chestnut pudding, 153, 175
grains, basic, 12
grapefruit, hot, 157
grapes: grapes and kiwi brûlée, 153, 176; guava, grape and mango delight, 154; kiwi, orange and grapes caramel in cream, 158, 172
Grecque, à la carrots, courgettes, mangetout, mushrooms, onions, 25, 174, 175, 176
guava: guava fool, 159; guava, grape and mango delight, 154; guava meringue, 163; winter fruit salad, 167, 173, 174, 175, 176

halumi cheese and egg, 34, 173
hamin eggs, 32, 172, 174
haricot beans, *see* beans
hazelnut and vegetable pilaf, 101, 175
herbs, 4; in larder, 13–14
honey: honey cake, 155, 173; yoghourt and honey, 168, 172
hummus, 35, 173, 175, 176

Jerusalem artichoke soup, 67

kiwi fruit: grapes and kiwi brûlée, 153, 176; kiwi, orange and grapes caramel in cream, 156, 172; kiwi meringue, 163; kiwi pavlova, 157–8; winter fruit salad, 167, 173, 174, 175, 176
knives, 9

lady's fingers, *see* okra
larder: basic stock, 11–14
leeks: leek and potato soup, 68; leeks
    croustade, 102; leeks à la Grecque,
    36, 174, 175, 176; leeks in tomato
    and garlic sauce, 37, 172, 175
lemon: baked bananas in lemon and rum
    sauce, 140, 175, 176; butter and
    lemon sauce, 17; celeriac in lemon
    sauce, 26
lemon squeezer, 10
lentils, 5; green or brown lentil soup,
    65; lentil hotpot, 103; lentil and
    tahini dip, 38; lentils with
    vegetables, 104–5, 176; red lentil
    soup, 76; winter warmer soup, 85,
    173
liquidiser, 8

main courses, 87–130
mangetout à la Grecque, 36
mango: guava, grape and mango
    delight, 154; mango fool, 159;
    mango meringue, 163; winter fruit
    salad, 167
marinade, for goat's cheese, 33
Marmite, 4
mayonnaise, 22
measures: equivalents, 7
melon: melon with port, 160, 172, 173,
    175, 176; winter fruit salad, 167
meringues: apple meringue, 139, 174;
    guava meringue, 163; chocolate
    meringue, 146, 173, 175; passion
    fruit meringue, 163, 173, 174, 175
minestrone soup, 69
miso, 5
mousse: chestnut mousse, 145, 174;
    chocolate mousse, 147, 173, 174,
    175; orange mousse, 162
mushrooms: courgettes and
    mushrooms in sour cream, 27;
    mushroom and curd cheese
    marjoram pie, 106, 174; mushroom
    and garlic soup, 70, 174;
    mushroom and garlic starter, 39,
    172, 174, 176; mushroom pilaf,
    109; mushroom stroganoff, 110,
    175, 176; mushrooms in filo pastry,
    107–8, 175; mushrooms à la
    Grecque, 36; spaghetti alla pirata,
    117; stuffed mushrooms, 43, 172, 175

nuts: apple and pistachio filo pastry,
    137–8; banana and nut pilaf, 91–2;
    cashew nut, vegetable and cheese
    flan, 95; chestnut casserole, 96;
    chestnut mousse, 145; figs,

yoghourt and nuts, 144; ginger
    chestnut pudding, 152; hazelnut
    and vegetable pilaf, 101; pecan
    pie, 164; stuffed artichokes, 120;
    yoghourt and honey, 168

oil, olive, 3–4
okra and tomato pilaf, 111, 172
olive oil, 3–4
olives: spaghetti alla pirata, 117
onions: egg and onion, 28, 173; onion
    soup, 71; onions à la Grecque, 36;
    parsnip and onion soufflé, 112–13,
    174; stuffed onions, 44, 174; tomato
    and onion soup, 80
orange: kiwi, orange and grapes
    caramel in cream, 156, 172;
    orange mousse, 162; oranges in
    caramel, 161, 172, 174

parsley 4
parsnip: cream of parsnip soup, 64, 176;
    parsnip and onion soufflé, 112–13,
    174; parsnips in garlic and
    breadcrumbs, 46; swede, parsnip,
    and turnip soup, 78
passion fruit meringue, 163, 173, 174,
    175
pasta: chick pea pasta, 97, 172; pasta
    and bean soup, 72; pasta and pepper
    sauce, 114, 172; spaghetti alla
    pirata, 117
pastry, filo, *see* filo pastry
pâtés: Brussels sprouts, 25, 174, 176;
    broccoli, 25; courgettes, 25; spinach,
    25
pavlova, kiwi, 157–8
pear fool, 159
peas: chick pea pasta, 97, 172; hummus,
    35, 173, 175, 176; mangetout à la
    Grecque, 36; pea soup, 73; winter
    warmer soup, 85, 173
pecan pie, 164
peppers: avocado and pepper spread,
    23, 172; pasta and pepper sauce,
    114, 172; stuffed peppers, 121–2,
    176
phillo pastry, *see* filo pastry
pies, *see* flans and pies
pilaf: banana and nut pilaf, 91–2;
    buckwheat and vegetable pilaf,
    94; hazelnut and vegetable pilaf,
    101, 175; mushroom pilaf, 109;
    okra and tomato pilaf, 111, 172
pine nuts: banana and nut pilaf, 91
pineapple: pineapple fool, 159;
    pineapple in rum, 165, 173, 175;
    winter fruit salad, 167, 173

turnip: swede, parsnip, and turnip soup, 78; turnips in garlic and breadcrumbs, 46, 174

vegetables. See also beans, potatoes, etc: barley and vegetable soup 56, 173; buckwheat and vegetable pilaf, 94; cashew nut, vegetable and cheese flan, 95, 173; couscous and vegetables, 98, 172; hazelnut and vegetable pilaf, 101, 175; lentil hotpot, 103; lentils with vegetables, 104–5, 176; minestrone soup, 69; mixed salad, 132; tofu Chinese style with vegetables, 126; vegetable antipasto with aioli, 47–8, 175; vegetable stroganoff, 127; winter quiche, 128–9; winter vegetable hors d'oeuvre, 50, 175; winter vegetable soup, 84; winter warmer casserole, 130, 173; winter warmer soup, 85, 173

vinaigrette, 24, 132
vine leaves, stuffed, 124–5

walnuts: banana and nut pilaf, 91
watercress: watercress eggs, 49, 175; watercress soup, 81; watercress and wine soup, 82, 176
wine: watercress and wine soup, 82, 176

yeast extract, 4
yoghourt, 5; figs, yoghourt and nuts, 144, 172; yoghourt and honey, 168, 172